When your kids aren't kids anymore

PARENTING LATE-TEEN AND ADULT CHILDREN

JERRY & MARY WHITE

NAVPRESS
A MINISTRY OF THE NAVIGATORS
P.O. BOX 6000, COLORADO SPRINGS, COLORADO 80934

The Navigators is an international Christian
organization. Jesus Christ gave His follow-
ers the Great Commission to go and make
disciples (Matthew 28:19). The aim of The
Navigators is to help fulfill that commission by
multiplying laborers for Christ in every nation.

NavPress is the publishing ministry of The
Navigators. NavPress publications are tools
to help Christians grow. Although publications alone cannot make disciples or change
lives, they can help believers learn biblical
discipleship, and apply what they learn to their
lives and ministries.

First printing, paperback edition, 1991

Unless otherwise noted, Scripture quotations
in this publication are from the *Holy Bible: New
International Version* (NIV). Copyright © 1973,
1978, 1984, International Bible Society. Used
by permission of Zondervan Bible Publishers.
Other versions used are the *New American
Standard Bible* (NASB), © The Lockman Foundation 1960, 1962, 1963, 1968, 1971, 1972,
1973, 1975, 1977; and *The Living Bible* (TLB),
© 1971 owned by assignment by the Illinois
Regional Bank N.A. (as trustee), used by
permission of Tyndale House Publishers, Inc.,
Wheaton, IL 60189.

Printed in the United States of America

Contents

Preface   9

Part I: Coming Out of the Cocoon (Ages 16-22)
   1. Parent's Preparation: Am I Ready for This?   13
   2. Communication: Are We Talking the Same
      Language?   25
   3. Moving Them Toward Independence   39
   4. Coaching Decision Making   59
   5. Guiding Career Preparation   73

Part II: Flying on Their Own (Ages 22+)
   6. Letting Go   91
   7. Boomerang Children: They Return   109
   8. Welcoming In-Laws and Grandchildren   123
   9. The Power of Influence   139
   10. Facing Difficult Times   151
   11. Healing the Past   169
   12. A Final Word   185
Endnotes   187

To our dearly loved adult children:
Steve and Julie White
Kathy and Dave Gray
Karen and Tim Birch
Kristin White

Authors

Jerry White is General Director of The Navigators. He holds
a Ph.D. in astronautics. During thirteen years with the United States Air Force, he served as a space mission controller
at Cape Canaveral. He also served as associate professor of
astronautics at the United States Air Force Academy for six
years, and co-authored a nationally recognized textbook on
astrodynamics. He resigned from active duty in 1973.

Mary Ann Knutson White attended Northwestern
Bible College and the University of Washington. She
holds a degree in English from the University of Colorado,
and has worked as a secretary in government and private
industry.

The Whites' first contact with The Navigators was at
the University of Washington. They later helped begin Nav-
igator ministries at the Air Force Academy in 1964 and at
Purdue University in 1966.

Jerry and Mary are the authors of *Friends and Friendship*.
Jerry has also written *Honesty, Morality, and Conscience*; and
The Power of Commitment.

Preface

When we were younger we were told, "Once a parent, always a parent." It didn't make sense. The kids grow up, marry and leave home, and we sail into the sunset enjoying our grandchildren and our recreational vehicle!

What a myth! What a rude awakening awaited us! We do keep on being parents, but without any of the classic authority and control of a parent with younger children. The issues become more complex and less manageable.

At this writing our children are 29, 27, 25, and 19. Three are married. We are right in the middle of the task of *parenting adult children*. So what are we doing writing a book about it? At times, we wondered that also, as we faced many personal challenges in our own family. Perhaps we should wait until they are older and the tests of time refine our thoughts.

However, there is something about sharing life in progress that gives the viewpoint of a fellow learner and pilgrim. Our empathy is great because we are in the middle of this parenting period. We do not consider ourselves successful and right. It is uncomfortably clear to us that we make many mistakes. We realize that we can never stop growing as parents. We also find that all the "pat" answers of our younger years crumble under the reality of the present. Our suggestions are now more tempered and tentative than when we were looking at our elders going through hard times with their older children.

The principles and ideas in this book come from the truth of the Bible, from the many parents we have interviewed and interacted with, and from our own growing experiences. The thirty couples in our "Parents of Teens" class at our church labored with us through this material for many months, giving us valuable, firsthand insights and experiences. We have been careful in using our own children as examples. The lack of negative examples regarding them reflects our commitment not to expose them publicly. We are happy to explore our own mistakes, but they have private lives of their own. They have read and approved the manuscript. We have also been careful to disguise some illustrations to protect those who graciously shared their hurts, griefs, and mistakes with us. We have purposely combined or altered specific events to protect these people and still communicate the ideas.

This is an unfinished work, for we are unfinished at our parenting task. We pray that as you read and consider these thoughts you will be encouraged and enabled in the pilgrimage of parenting your adult children.

PART I
Coming Out of the Cocoon
Ages 16-22

1

Parent's Preparation: Am I Ready for This?

Butterflies are beautiful. Caterpillars are strange, but tolerable. But cocoons? They are an indiscriminate blob of unattractive materials. But out of the blob comes a beautiful butterfly—transformed from the ugly caterpillar.

As the butterfly nears the time to break out of the cocoon, it begins a fierce struggle to split the shell. Hoping to help the butterfly in its struggle, one person interceded by breaking the cocoon so the butterfly could escape more quickly. The butterfly fell to the ground, unable to fly. The process of breaking the cocoon strengthens the muscles necessary for the butterfly to fly. The well-meaning help actually destroyed the butterfly.

Similarly, there is no way the building of the cocoon can be hurried for the caterpillar. At its perfect time the transformation begins.

Teenagers are like that. They transform from child to adult. They do it according to their God-ordained timetable, not ours. Some begin at fourteen, others at seventeen. Some begin to fly at sixteen, others wait until twenty. Like different species of butterflies, each teen obeys his or her own inner timetable determined by sex, physical development, emotional growth, home environment, educational background, peer relationships, spiritual responses, and many other indefinable factors.

No computer can program them. No special delivery letter tells the parents, or the teen, that the cocoon is beginning or ending. Part of the mystery of this time of change is not knowing what is going on. One thing is certain—whether the transformation be smooth or tumultuous, it is inevitable.

The burgeoning young adult is highly influenceable. Unlike the butterfly that struggles on its own in the darkness of its cocoon, the young adult lives out his or her struggle in a transparent cocoon, open for all to see and few to fully understand. The struggles of this period determine much of his or her adult direction and accomplishment. No other time is so determinative, except for the highly impressionable preschool years.

Unlike the butterfly, the young adult interacts with people and the world during the entire process. Those outside forces are one of the ingredients in the transformation. And of all the influences, that of parents is very significant in molding the young adult, even though at the time parents may think they have lost complete contact. In silence and estrangement, or in the noise of conflict, the forming adult values of the young adult undergo testing and development. His or her adult behavior begins to set like drying concrete.

The characteristics of this period are as varied as fingerprints—many similarities, but each a unique experience. Rebellion, drugs, alcohol, sex, conflict, and premature independence are but a few of the negative possibilities. Compassion, concern, thoughtfulness, new goals, life purpose, self-assessment, achievement, love, and stability are some of the positive outcomes.

Many fine books have been written on raising teenagers. It is not our intent to add to that collection. We will include many common aspects of raising teens, but our focus is on the later teen years, when they have become young adults. We want to emphasize the process of helping them to develop as responsible adults, and the parent's changing role and responsibility in that process.

We see this in two distinct phases loosely defined by ages sixteen to twenty-two and twenty-two to thirty *plus*. The first section discusses ages sixteen to twenty-two where adolescence concludes, adulthood starts, independence begins, many life decisions are made, education and careers interface, adult singleness predominates, and they finally leave home. This person is described better by events than by age. It is a time of breaking out and breaking away.

The inaugural lesson of this period is that *life is not simple*. It is, in fact, difficult and complex. Life is fraught with problems, hard decisions, emotional traumas, and uncertainty.

As older adults we understand this. But do we remember the turmoil of that time in our own lives? We generally exercise selective memories, recalling only the outstanding pains and pleasures of our teen years.

Reflect on those years of your own life. Remember those conflicts, fears, fantasies, and feelings of awkwardness and uncertainty. Remember the peer pressures, the guilt of giving in to temptation, the discovery of your sexual self, the first loves—and the first heartbreaks. Remember the sin you struggled with or committed. Recall your feelings toward your parents, brothers, and sisters. Relive the memory of your anger, hurts, embarrassments, and loneliness.

But also remember the times of feeling good—the successes and achievements, reaching goals, loving, being loved in return, the first kiss, the first date. Remember the secrets you never told your parents.

If you were sexually experienced before marriage,

remember the inner struggles, the guilt, and even the elation of the experience. Bring back the memory of the struggles that resulted from sexual decisions. Or your experience with alcohol or drugs. Or your thoughts about suicide.

Many of these memories are not pleasant, but they are real. In dredging them up, we may be able to develop more empathy for what our young adult is experiencing. Take time to write out a few of the major events and feelings of your late teens and early twenties. Feel them again in your mind and emotions.

One part of us desperately wants to protect our sons and daughters from the hurts and mistakes of *our* past. Another part wants to mandate upon them our successes and values and to force them to learn from the hard times we experienced.

But this is impossible. The world has changed. Their environment is different from what ours was. They don't live on a farm, walk two miles to school in a blizzard, carry newspapers for a dollar a week, or experience any of the legendary hardships we did. Our past can never be their present. But our feelings of the past can mirror their feelings now. The specifics differ, but the inner turmoil is similar. To some degree, even their personalities will bear resemblance to ours.

Conflict, internal and external, is normal during this period. Young adults struggle against restraints while attempting to find their own personhood, yet they fear what they will find. Arguments and misunderstandings, both in the family and with other adults and friends, are part of the process. How else will they learn to speak up for their beliefs and to resolve conflict? How else can they see the damage of anger and thoughtless words in an adult world unless they experience it in the forgiving atmosphere of the home?

Put yourself in their place. Feel their pain. Struggle with

them. They may never acknowledge that you understand, but in your heart you can know that you have felt with them. In fact, *feeling* is a key word. They do not want explanations, logic, or reason. They long for you to feel what they feel. As difficult as it is to feel another's hurts, we can try. We can empathize. We want an open door to their hearts, not just their minds.

Just in case our young adults have been totally cooperative, exhibiting minimal negative traits, do not ignore the fact that they *do experience inner turmoil*, whether they express it or not. Often what is bottled up will emerge in later life.

ARE WE PREPARED?

Are we prepared? The answer is a categorical no. For most of us our only preparation for nurturing this young adult in our home is our personal experience. And it is inadequate. For one thing, it is only one experience, vaguely remembered and rarely based on principles. Additionally, what fit us or helped us may not even remotely fit our sons and daughters.

When our four children came to this point in life, we were totally unprepared and frequently perplexed. And we were reasonably conscientious parents. How we wish we had asked advice of older couples or known where to seek help! But we didn't. Now that our four children are in the eighteen-to-thirty-plus age group, we have even more questions. But we are learning. We do not believe that we have done, or are doing, everything well. Consequently, we are drawing upon the experiences of many other parents in formulating this book.

How can *you* be better prepared? We suggest that you:

- study and analyze your own experiences during this period of life;

- study and analyze what your parents did;
- learn from the experience of others, both positive and negative;
- formulate a few basic principles to guide you in your interaction with your adult children;
- seek wisdom and direction from God; and
- admit your own need to change and grow.

Ask God to change you as He changes them. Give yourself to God in a new way for the sake of your adult children. At this point you know you no longer *control* them. Your only hope is to influence them through your life.

But wait! Don't get the idea that this period of life will be miserable. It's exciting! What greater reward can parents receive than to see their children break out of that confusing cocoon and emerge as beautiful, confident adults? It is a process that will deepen our relationship with them and with God.

At the time our oldest children were born, fathers seldom observed a baby's birth. Even mothers were often asleep or groggy during the process. Today parents share the miracle of watching their infant struggling into the world, covered with blood and mucus, wriggling and crying. The parents are oblivious to all but the incredible exhilaration of the moment. A new life. Unlimited potential. A joyful fulfillment of their love.

The young adult transformation has all the same miraculous characteristics. It's exhilarating. But, like childbirth, it can be painful, messy, and traumatic. In childbirth, the mother participates actively, but the baby comes regardless of her efforts and attitude. With the young adult, we are also participants—hopefully active ones. But the transformation will happen with or without us.

Throughout this book we will suggest many things you

can do to prepare yourself spiritually, emotionally, and practically for this time. We will try to be your guide, encourager, and counselor at each stage. But only you can actually place yourself in the inner circle of your young adult's life. Do it! Take the risk!

THE GOAL

What should be our goal as our young adults grow through this process of leaving the cocoon to flying on their own? Survival? Abandonment? Control? None of these, we hope. Rather, we want them to become all that they can be as mature adults. Life is filled with examples of parents who interfere, intimidate, criticize, or otherwise cause grief for young people trying to emerge as independent persons. Some of the most difficult emotional hassles for young people emanate from relationships with their parents. Consider this as a sample goal:

> *Our overall goal for our sons and daughters is that they
> grow into mature, independent, godly adults
> who base their lives on sound principles,
> who are emotionally and spiritually strong,
> who have a strong sense of responsibility toward their
> fellowman,
> who will face good and difficult times with calmness
> and perseverance, and
> who, if married, become competent and faithful
> husbands, wives, and parents.*

Though this may be a noble goal, we must recognize that we, as parents, cannot control the outcome of our young adults' lives. They are in command of their own lives. A parent may be a virtual model of parenting and yet see his or her offspring stray from God, become unstable, and generally be immature and irresponsible in life. This is their choice. One couple told us with deep sadness, "Our son shows all the biblical characteristics of a fool." We can influence them by life and prayer. We can do only what they allow us to do. We must not give up or fail to try to influence them.

Another dilemma arises when they make decisions or develop values that we do not agree with, but that we do not believe to be wrong, immoral, or ungodly either. They *must* have freedom to do this—in fact they must be clearly, *even verbally*, granted this freedom. *There are no rubber-stamp kids! There are no perfect parents!*

Not one of us could claim that his or her values, beliefs, and principles of living are the only valid ones. Just as we broke away from, developed different values and traditions from, and even criticized our parents, so will our offspring. We want them to be deeper, smarter, more wise and godly, and more principled than we ever were. Remember that one day we will be dependent on them. They will be the future leaders of the Church, the community, the nation, and the society.

THE PARENT'S MIND-SET

Logic seldom reigns in the heat of an argument. Good principles are rarely formed on the spur of the moment. Right actions do not result automatically without forethought, prayer, and preparation. So logic, principles, and right actions on the part of parents need foundations and preparation. This book or any other set of suggestions will be of little value without one major ingredient—*your mind-set*.

Mind-set is the "set of our mind"—how we think. It is the settled opinion deep within our being based on the complex mix of experience, beliefs, background, and knowledge. Our mind-set will influence the strength of our relationship and the depth of our interaction with our young adults.

Like cholesterol that builds up in the human arteries, some of these "settled opinions" need to be broken up and stirred to permit new thinking to occur. Yet we have found that our old ideas, our prejudices, and the pride of our past decisions and experiences are so very hard to overcome.

Should we as parents abandon our past, our wisdom, our deepest values, or our considered opinions of life? Certainly not. But we must consciously work at changing our mind-set in several ways.

We need to be *learners*. A closed mind is a tragedy. The older we get the easier it is to think that we are learners when we really are not. We say we are, but only in certain areas—those that do not cross our preconceived notions.

One major theme of the book of Proverbs is seeking wisdom. Proverbs 1:5 tells us that "a wise man will hear and increase in learning, and a man of understanding will acquire wise counsel" (NASB). Being a learner does not mean abandoning truth and personal conviction. It does mean opening personal ideas to challenge and change when prejudice or faulty thinking are uncovered. It means hearing another person's point of view, listening honestly, and truly understanding his or her thinking.

Listening and learning do not require agreement, as the author of Proverbs implies: "Give instruction to a wise man and he will be still wiser, teach a righteous man, and he will increase his learning" (Proverbs 9:9, NASB). Verse 8 has just said, "Do not reprove a scoffer, lest he hate you." Are we willing to be corrected and taught?

Many times as a father I have argued with my young adult children and brought great frustration upon them.

Something inside me welled up when their views opposed mine, and I determined to *prove* my point, which I often did since I argue well verbally. I crunched them and beat them down verbally. But often I was not willing to truly listen and learn from them. I won, but I lost. Finally one of them confronted me on my way of arguing. I was ashamed at my pride and insensitivity. Even now, I find the old habits of verbal bombardment rising when one of my daughters or my son expresses an opinion opposed to mine, but I am trying to change.

Strangely, we are often more willing to learn from others, even those the age of our young adults, than we are from our own sons and daughters. However, we *can* learn from them. We *need* to learn from them about the world *they* live in with its values, pressures, and realities.

We need to be *willing to change* our thinking to fit the reality of their world. We need to change when our thinking is shown to be faulty.

We need a mind-set to *admit our mistakes*. All of us have made mistakes in raising our children. Part of being a learner is to be able to admit our mistakes to ourselves and to our young adults.

We need a mind-set to *let them be their own persons*. It is hard to let go and let them be themselves. That will happen regardless of what we do. But we must make that an integral part of our thinking—to participate in the process, not to hinder it.

When we interact with our teenagers or young adults we *must avoid an "I'm right, you're wrong" attitude*. They sense that quickly. They need to know we come to them with an open mind. That is not easy. Parents often are right, but they must not prejudge the situation.

Finally, we need to adopt a mind-set that uncouples our pride and ego from their actions. Specifically, *do not tie their success or failure to your ego.* We must not live our lives vicariously through them.

Our children wondered at times why we pushed them so hard for good grades and success in sports, music, or spiritual activities. It is as though they said, "Do you want this for me or for you? Are you more concerned for your own reputation than for me?" Even as young adults they wonder about our motives.

It only takes one young adult in a family who rebels, takes drugs, becomes ill, or is seriously hurt in an accident to bring all our "success thinking" into a perspective of what really counts in life. We must want the best for them, not for ourselves. They must know we will openly and willingly identify ourselves with them no matter what they achieve or what mistakes they make.

CONCLUSIONS

In so many ways, we are spectators watching this fascinating emergence from the cocoon as our young adults vacillate between childhood and adult life. We watch from the sidelines and occasionally during brief times have the opportunity to rush in and give them a hug, a word of encouragement, a look of approval, a word of counsel, or even a Band-Aid for their wound. They are no longer children. They are moving into a life of their own. But they do look back to see if we approve, if there is still that refuge of love—just in case.

2

Communication: Are We Talking the Same Language?

During a recent Christmas holiday, one of our daughters returned from college. She found me in the kitchen one morning in a hurried frenzy of cooking preparations for expected guests. She watched for a few moments and then said, "Mom, you seem awfully tense. Do you want to know a good way to handle pressure?"

Under the stress of the moment, I snapped, "Please, don't analyze me now. I'm busy." A hurt look crossed her face and she left the kitchen. I felt smitten at the needless hurt I had caused. I followed her and asked her forgiveness, which she graciously gave. But she didn't offer again to tell me her suggestion for handling pressure (which I obviously needed!), and I don't blame her. I wouldn't risk it either.

Parents probably make more mistakes in the area of communication than any other aspect of their relationship to young adults. Relationships grow out of communication. Some is nonverbal, of course, but the way we speak and the specific words we speak set the tone for interaction with our young adults.

We all live with regrets and self-condemnation for things we have said, for responses made in anger and frustration. But words once spoken cannot be recalled. They live forever in the minds of those who hear them.

Any parent could tell of many words spoken in haste and regretted for a lifetime. A small, thoughtless statement quickly said is impossible to retrieve and can devastate trust and intimacy. Perhaps Solomon had spoken rashly to one of his sons or daughters when he wrote, "Reckless words pierce like a sword, but the tongue of the wise brings healing" (Proverbs 12:18). Words pierce, wound, and infect or soothe, heal, and build. They are not neutral.

Conflicts and misunderstandings rule some homes, while in more peaceful families harsh words only occasionally invade conversations. Parents who have enjoyed amiable friendships with younger teens are often dismayed to find themselves embroiled in disputes and struggles with young adults who are battling their way toward independence. These hostilities vary in intensity, but most parents would admit to some significant disagreements as their young adults prepare to leave. When this happens we need to ask these questions:

- Are these clashes inevitable?
- Can parents talk with teens without conflict?
- Can important issues be discussed?
- What convinces a young adult to really listen?
- Do parents respect the opinions of their young adults?
- What issues are really important to discuss?
- Who should initiate serious conversations?
- Who is responsible for setting the tone of conversations?

No parent, or young adult either, wants or enjoys division and fighting. We have seen parents weep as they relate the strained distance that separates them from their young adult. Yet we know teenagers who desperately long to be heard and understood and accepted. Why then, with this yearning for harmony on both sides, do we experience so much division and discord? Are there ways to avoid much of the quarreling that disrupts and poisons families during these years?

Young adults change and mature so rapidly during these years that many parents find themselves left behind in knowing the right communication skills. We are essentially conversing with adults, a fact so easy to forget. One of our college-aged daughters rightfully criticized us: "You're talking to me like I'm still a little kid." So true. So easy to do. Yet so hurtful.

Our young adults deserve all the respect, courtesy, and attention we would give any adult in conversation. We tread a fine line because we still bear parental responsibilities with them, and they bear obligations to us, significantly complicating the relationship. But when we fully realize they have attained at least some degree of independence, our style in relating to them must change.

Most peacemaking efforts should come from the parents. They have had many more years to mature, to gain understanding, to learn how to listen, to follow the advice given by James in his epistle: "My dear brothers, take note of this: Everyone should be quick to listen, slow to speak and slow to become angry" (James 1:19).

If, as parents, we haven't yet learned to listen with understanding, we can start as our teens reach the crucial years of young adulthood. One of our daughters used to say to us with her hand chopping the air, "Would you listen, would you *please* just listen?"

The habits of communication formed as our teens gain independence establish patterns for years to come, even for a lifetime. We must be the first to apologize for cruel, thoughtless words. We must pay attention even when we would rather be doing something else. We must tolerate foolish statements and wild ideas without ridicule in return, and we must gently lead them to a wiser way of thinking.

How often have we listened with little attention and no attempt to understand. "Dad, Mom, you don't understand!" is true. How can we understand what we do not really hear?

Poor communication with sons and daughters in their late teens can potentially destroy relationships and tear families apart. The restoration process can be long and painful, maybe never taking place at all. Far better to make an effort to change as they gain independence.

One young man, now married and a father of small children, said, "My dad died last year, and almost every time I remember him, I think about the way he talked to me when I was growing up. When he was angry, which seemed to be most of the time, he would start his conversations with me by saying, 'Listen, you stupid idiot. . . .' I try to get that out of my mind, but whenever I have to tackle a hard job at work, it seems I automatically think I'm a stupid idiot."

How tragic! What a poisonous heritage! Our words are heard and remembered, especially the negative ones. We must guard our words with care and prayer, building, not destroying, their fragile egos.

HOW TO COMMUNICATE

Show a Right Attitude

Good communication never begins with the spoken word, but rather with the attitude of the one speaking. We all know the importance of giving full attention to our young adults as they speak, giving them eye contact, allowing no interruptions, and responding courteously.

However, when subjects are painful, embarrassing, or intensely personal, direct eye contact is occasionally too intimidating for young people. A lengthy walk in the park or a leisurely drive will give them a chance to express themselves without constantly watching the parent's face for an immediate reaction. The key is the interest and attention, not necessarily direct eye contact.

Our communication quickly lets our young adults know our attitude toward them. They perceive if we are judgmental and critical. They sense compassion, acceptance, concern, and caring.

Choose Subjects with Care

Often parents feel desperate to share their experienced knowledge with their young adults, but we lose a hearing because they know we are nagging, contentious, or domineering. We have learned many things they desperately need to hear, but they may not listen if they sense force and frustration behind our words.

We may want to communicate the dangers of speeding on the highway, but because we tell them so often, they soon tune us out. We insist so frequently that they have personal devotionals that they close down their minds even if they agree.

At our stage of life, and theirs, we need to choose issues and words with care. It's true that we have learned much about life, and we want to spare them the trauma of learning the hard way. But that may not be the best for them, so verbal restraint is the wisest policy we can follow. As Solomon tells us, "When words are many, sin is not absent, but he who holds his tongue is wise" (Proverbs 10:19).

Listen and Understand

Not only must we restrict how much we say, but our words must be liberally interspersed with genuine listening. Listening is paramount. We can listen even when we can't agree. Our young adults have lived with us long enough to have a good idea of what our responses will be to many of the subjects they want to discuss. It is hard to break those patterns in their minds.

Then too, when they are feeling hostile or angry, not necessarily with us as their parents, they may choose to vent their frustrations on us with provocative statements and language. Even then we must be willing to listen and try to hear the cry behind the words, the deep feelings that they rarely express, especially to parents.

Interruptions effectively destroy communication. Even when young adults share wild and crazy things, they deserve the courtesy of a hearing. One college student told us, "My mom always listens. I know she doesn't always agree, but she never makes fun of me or my ideas. Eventually, she'll let me know what she thinks, but she always hears me out first." Solomon advised as much when he wrote, "He who answers before listening—that is his folly and his shame" (Proverbs 18:13).

After a frightening nightmare about death, one of our children once asked us, "What if all the people who don't believe in God are right? What if there isn't a Heaven?"

Those penetrating, thought-provoking questions needed more than flippant answers about faith. We spent weeks dialoguing within the family—many late night talks about deep, eternal values. If we had glossed over the questions with quick, unsatisfying answers, that teen's faith could have been shaken for years. It's frightening to think that we may have opted for easy answers or no answers at all because of our hectic schedules, fatigue, irritability, or impatience. We may not know the answers. We can say so. Honesty and a helpful attitude are what we need.

If our young adults realize that our listening is coupled

with a longing to *understand*, we are more free to disagree without losing the relationship. One of our young adults has chosen a political posture that is different from ours. We have had many interesting discussions, sometimes quite heated, yet free of antagonism, during which we do not try to convince one another but attempt to understand. Political discussions can offer neutral ground for listening and understanding because little of a personal nature is involved.

Sometimes parents spend hours listening to trivial conversation before real thoughts and feelings are verbalized. One of our daughters enjoys having her back scratched. While one of us is doing that we will ask her how things are going with her. She will often say, "Well, just ask me some questions." A few simple questions give her a chance to share openly and deeply about her life. Back-scratching doesn't work for everyone, but some form of relaxing time does.

This is the time of life to make caring evident. Coaching and counsel will have a place, but let caring predominate.

Our teenagers may be going through a terrible phase, perhaps facing some horrendous predicament, and there may not be another human being in the world attempting to understand. Again, let us emphasize that understanding does not mean agreeing or approving of behavior or ideas, but attempting to get inside the minds and spirits of our young adults to grasp how they feel. Not many parents do this well. To our regret, we have failed many times. It's so time-consuming and energy-draining that many parents give up before they reach that depth of relationship with their sons and daughters.

Avoid Cutting Remarks

Sharp retorts and cutting gibes will only halt further communication. If we can restrain our responses until the situation calms down, we have a chance to work through broken communication and gain insight into our young adults' feelings and thoughts. Most adults are masters of cutting remarks. They have had years of practice. The tragedy is that the pain and scars of those remarks linger for so long in the minds of our young adults. Solomon wrote in Proverbs 13:3, "He who guards his lips guards his life, but he who speaks rashly will come to ruin."

Refuse Verbal Abuse

There is a limit. No parent should tolerate a barrage of malicious, vindictive mistreatment from anyone, least of all his or her young adult offspring. Although emotional outbursts are common during the pressured days of approaching adulthood, parents don't have to accept constant harangues and discourteous behavior. As we would with anyone who is rude, we can say, "I refuse to talk to you now. I will not accept verbal abuse from you," and then leave.

One father described appalling shouting matches with his oldest son—arguments that tore at the whole family and wedged a rift between him and his wife. The son would scream in anger at any family member who crossed his path. The father, especially, bore the brunt of the son's uncontrolled rage. The situation seemed hopeless until the father told the son that he refused to talk with him until they could do so in normal tones. The hostile silence would sometimes exist for days between them. But eventually the son realized his outbursts were futile. Finally, after several years, they were able to talk calmly and even with friendship.

Learn from Them

We can learn from what our teens are thinking about: how they are being influenced by their peers, in what ways they perceive the world differently than we do, how deep their spiritual life is. Young people today think deeply about issues that were distant and vague to us at their age. They face serious and frightening aspects of life from which we were protected by the comparative innocence of society a generation ago.

Through our young adults, we are able to learn about the world of today and the influences that mold and control them. Learning from our teens will foster greater understanding and communication between us.

Many times we feel baffled and confused by the sudden shifts in their thinking patterns, and by the bizarre ideas they seem to have adopted as their own. Rather than cutting off communication by ridiculing their ideas, leave the door open for further discussion by saying, "That's interesting. I would like to think about that some more before I comment." Or, "I had never considered that idea. I'm not sure I agree, but let me think it over." Or, "Could you tell me some of the thinking you have done to reach that conclusion? I would really be interested."

In other areas such as lifestyle choices, spiritual decisions, and moral choices, we usually have ample opportunity to listen with understanding and learn from them before making our own feelings and opinions known. In many cases they think they already know our views and opinions. Surprise them by restraint and thoughtful interaction.

Protect Confidences

A truly crucial aspect of communication is the ability to keep confidences that our young adults share with us. If they ask us to keep any information confidential and we break that trust, we may never restore the relationship fully. Solomon tells us that "a gossip betrays a confidence, but a trustworthy man keeps a secret" (Proverbs 11:13). When a young adult shares a confidence with either mother or father, she or he should request permission before sharing it with the other parent. In that way trust is deepened.

But even under the best of circumstances communication with young adults carries overtones of past conversations to such an extent that our attempts to "do it right" can be drowned out. This problem comes from two directions. Whenever we speak, whatever we say bears a coded message from the past. We say one thing, they hear another.

"I understand" might be interpreted "I don't understand." "That's a good idea" might be interpreted "That's a dumb idea. I don't agree." "Tell me about it" might be interpreted "I don't trust you." "Why did you . . . ?" might be interpreted "You blew it again." "Here's a suggestion" might be interpreted "Do it this way."

Each statement bears its own history from the past—a meaning far beyond words. It may take some time for young adults to realize that we are truly trying to change our communication to openness and honesty.

Thus, communication is not just an application of technique. One person can do only so much. The receiver must also perceive that the communication is sincere. The best communication must still be received and believed.

WHAT TO COMMUNICATE

Parents have plenty that they want to communicate to their children—most of it based on a strong urge to change their children's behavior or ideas.

But once our children have reached adulthood, we need to choose our topics carefully, especially if we are disapproving in our words or attitudes. We will have a limited amount of time to communicate, and we don't want to waste that time on trivial subjects or unprofitable nagging.

We're not speaking here of the ordinary, everyday

communication that goes on in every family regarding daily activities, the weather, and the trivia of life. We all communicate in that way, and it provides a comfortable backdrop for deeper communication. Rather, we are speaking of those times when the mood turns serious and our young adults share with us on a deep level. We need God's wisdom and patience to keep the communication lines open and flowing from the parent's heart to theirs and back again. As the Apostle Paul tells us in Ephesians 4:29, "Do not let any unwholesome talk come out of your mouths, but only what is helpful for building others up according to their needs, that it may benefit those who listen."

Carefully pick areas to emphasize. Be willing to give up on the little things, or as young adults have said, "Don't sweat the small stuff." If we constantly criticize their music choices, will they listen to us about ethical issues? If we nag three times a day about hair in the bathroom sink, will they respond when we want to discuss substance abuse? If we belittle their fashion choices, will we win a hearing about obedience to God? We want them to hear us when we talk about these important areas:

- Marriage and fidelity
- Ethics
- Biblical morality
- Spiritual foundations
- Character concerns
- Relationships

Let insignificant things slide. Concentrate on the majors of life, not the minors. Offer praise and commendation often. Emphasize their strong points much more than their weaknesses, and build their confidence with sincere verbal tributes.

While flexibility and understanding are important, there are areas in which we must stand firm. Direct scriptural commands, moral convictions, ethical standards, and personal principles aren't open for discussion. Arguments in these areas are never profitable. We may have to make statements like the following: "You are attacking my personal principles. I can't back down on that." "I can't control your thinking, but I have made a decision before God for myself." "I'll think about your point of view, but my initial reaction is that I can't agree." "Your statements downgrade my convictions, and I can't see any reason to continue with this discussion."

Since young adults, indeed some people, crusade to change everyone else's opinions to conform to their own, they seem possessed by an undeniable need for everyone to authenticate their opinions. Such people end their dogmatic statements with phrases like these: "Don't you agree?" "Can't you see I'm right?" and "What I've said is right, isn't it?"

If you are the parents of such a person, you already recognize the strength of his or her determination. Don't be bullied into endless discussions that lead nowhere. Simply end the dialogue and move to another topic.

Again, let us emphasize the importance of *choosing* areas of importance to communicate to each *individual* young adult. Keep in mind that those issues will change rapidly as the young adult's environment, friendships, and experiences alter from year to year, or even month to month.

Sometimes, no matter how diligently a parent seeks to communicate and dialogue with a son or daughter, that teen simply will not respond. Such silence may be due to hostility, a reserved personality, obstinacy, shyness, an adolescent phase, or just plain perverseness. In any case, parents cannot force conversation. Patience, courtesy, and time *may* bring about good communication in the future, but there are no guarantees.

CONCLUSIONS

Good communication is built on the foundation blocks of love, trust, listening, and understanding. Even so, parents have no guarantees that the response will be in kind. Every person chooses his or her own attitudes and responses. We can be encouraged as we remember that our relationships with our young adults are in *process* and we are building for a lifetime of communication with them.

3

Moving Them Toward Independence

Solo. On your own. I remember my first solo flight in an airplane. I was twenty, in college, and learning to fly in a Cessna 150. The big event was my first solo flight. The instructor has to judge when the student is prepared to fly alone with reasonable safety. I was an average flyer—certainly no Lindbergh! I dreamed about that solo with both anticipation and fear.

In the midst of one lesson the instructor told me to stop the plane just off the runway. She got out and said, "It's all yours." I knew it was coming, but it still caught me by surprise. With sweaty palms and a nervous stomach I took off, circled the field, and made the landing approach. The instructor stood by and watched, probably wondering if she had made the right decision. But once up in the air only I could land the plane. And land it I did, a landing that more likely resembled a controlled crash. At age twenty, I little realized what could have happened, for at that age life seemed eternal and indestructible.

Thirty years later at age fifty, I again flew a new airplane alone. A friend took me up in his French-built single-engine plane. I had not flown for over four years. I tried six landings with him with numerous small errors. Then he left for another city and told me to fly anytime I wanted. He didn't have time to watch me solo. I planned to fly the next morning.

I dreamed about it all night. I knew I could do it, yet now I was thirty years smarter and knew I was not indestructible. Again there was anticipation and fear. The next morning the flying went well, yet I admit I did sweat that first solo landing.

We all remember those first solo experiences—the first day in school, the first time driving a car, our first real date, a performance at church or school, marriage, our first child—and leaving home.

Every young adult looks forward to that time of independence and dreams of it, especially in the midteens. Although few can bring themselves to admit it, there is also the natural fear of the unknown. At age twenty would I ever admit to being afraid to fly solo? Never. So also a young adult hides the fear and outwardly pushes for independence.

There is a major difference between flying solo from parents and other solos. One *chooses* to fly, sing, date, or drive. In leaving home there is no choice. A young adult must become independent or live with an unhealthy adult dependence, which cripples and ultimately prevents maturity.

Independence is inevitable. But the timing, means, and circumstances are choices made by both parents and young adults. Sometimes these choices are cooperative and pleasant. Sometimes they are laced with conflict, anger, and bitterness. The purpose of this discussion is to help us as parents facilitate that move to independence as smoothly and naturally as possible.

Timing is of great importance. Too early a push to independence may cause young adults to "crash and burn," greatly damaging their self-confidence. Too late a push usually results in heightened conflict or unhealthy dependence.

But how does a parent know when it is too early or too late?

Each young adult differs in terms of maturity, personality, experience, and needs. Like an instructor pilot, parents need to carefully observe and evaluate when the right time emerges. Unlike the instructor, who has had many students and much experience, we parents have only a few chances to observe and try. Thus, we must learn all we can from the Scriptures, our own parents, and our peers.

Let's make the situation even more complex. How independent should the young adults be? In what areas? How soon? Certainly, independence is not an all-at-once matter. Few young adults could stand that shock of change. The new pilot first learns to take off and land safely. Navigation, instrument flying, and many other useful and important topics are developed in due time. Young adults, whenever possible, need staging and phasing into independence. Admittedly, some take matters into their own hands and force themselves into it all at once. But that is their choice, and they must live with it.

We propose three basic areas in which young adults should develop mature independence: *spiritual, emotional,* and *functional.* They need spiritual independence to make their beliefs their own, to form a basis for life decisions, and to have their own walk with God. They need emotional independence to become healthy, fulfilled adults who live lives apart from crippling emotional crutches. They need functional independence in the practical areas of living apart from the props and supports of their parental homes.

THE PROCESS

Growth never moves forward evenly, but by leaps and spurts with intermittent periods of tranquility. Growth into independence is a process for both the parents and young adults.

Events can be hurried, but the true process cannot be rushed. Even abrupt decisions or conflicts that force independence only throw the young adult into necessarily making independent decisions and actions, but the process of truly *being* independent as a person still takes time.

The parental part in this process can be summed up in four words: control, coaching, counsel, and caring.

Control is the use of authority and direct influence in a son or daughter's life and decisions. It is appropriate in childhood, but only of limited use in the teen years. During the years of control the authority clearly resides with the parent.

Coaching is the next stage. It should be entered as early as possible and in as many areas as possible. Coaching involves some authority. The coach guides, teaches, reprimands, and corrects—but the young adult is alone responsible to follow the coaching. Coaching is stronger than counsel, giving more detailed and ongoing guidance. Coaching may or may not be asked for.

Counsel is a natural outgrowth of good coaching. On a football team a young quarterback is first controlled by his coach, who calls all the plays. As the player gains experience, coaching replaces control, and it is less directive yet authoritative in instruction. Finally, a mature, experienced quarterback calls almost all his own plays, but with counsel as needed and requested from his coach. Counsel can never be forced. A young adult must ask for it. It is advice with no authority or strings attached.

Caring is the culmination of a successful process of parenting adult children. You care, you love—not demanding anything in return. Your adult offspring recognize your care and concern and respond to it with respect and honor. At times they ask for this care to be expressed in counsel or in coaching. But we initiate neither, allowing them the total freedom of choice. We now impact their lives on the basis of love and influence.

No clear line of demarcation separates these elements of the parenting process. They blend both in time and in specific areas. Simultaneously, you may counsel a young adult on his or her choice of school courses and sports, coach him or her on financial matters, and control her or him on the use of the family automobile. Thus the process varies with age, maturity, and specific areas of concern.

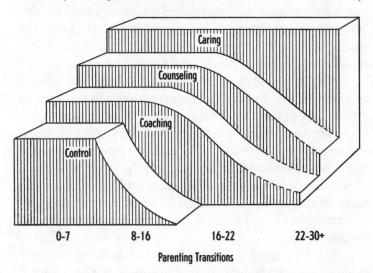

Parenting Transitions

We will return to these four basic elements of the parenting process many times in this book, since your knowledge of where you are in that process can be one of the most liberating factors in parenting your adult children.

Spiritual Independence

In our society we see groups of teenagers cast unwillingly into independence. They are "throwaway children," "latch-key kids," "urban castaways," "runaways," or children of drug addicts and alcoholics. What chance do they have? No parent cares for them. They face life alone and lonely.

In some respects, Joseph, the son of Jacob (Genesis 35-40), was a teenager like that. Joseph was a favored child, raised in a polygamous family, disliked by jealous brothers. In his teens he was sold by his brothers as a slave to a band of roving traders who later resold him in Egypt. There he had no one to guide him—no one to control, coach, counsel, or care. Yet on his own he decided to live for God. He made his own wise spiritual choices. He had the background of faith from the Jewish home of his father, Jacob. He knew the basics, but was on his own. He determined his own financial, sexual, and spiritual choices—and God honored him.

We want to give our sons and daughters the kind of background that will prepare them to make good choices on their own. But note: It will ultimately be their choice.

Though our adult children will not be snatched from us as Joseph was, they will still be cast on their own to make independent spiritual decisions. Even if we provide them with the best spiritual training from birth, they must still make their own way spiritually. Some of their choices will lead to heartache and disaster. Some will lead to deep spiritual conviction.

Ann was raised in a godly, strict home, the eldest child in her family. In high school she strained against her parents' control. She refused to live in submission to their standards. She sneaked out for dates and experimented with alcohol and drugs. Finally, she married a young man with no college education or career direction. Her grieving parents offered a tentative blessing and prayed.

But this young man was what she needed. Through the godly influence of a friend, he began to follow God and to lead his wife to a new depth of spiritual commitment. Today they are effective, godly parents of four children—a joy to the parents who had grieved earlier.

Polly was almost a copy of Ann in terms of background and high school rebellion. She also experimented freely with alcohol and drugs—and probably sex. She would have flashes of repentance, but always went back to anger and rebellion. And there she remains.

In these two examples, both sets of parents prayed. Both did all they knew how to do. Yet one set of parents rejoices, while the other waits with aching hearts.

Another common event is the deadly slide into spiritual indifference. Bruce came from a Christian family. He experienced personal salvation while quite young and grew up as a model son—active in church and other religious activities. In college he slid into lazy spiritual habits. He went to church sporadically but did little else in terms of spiritual growth.

He married a Christian girl, to the delight of his parents. As he entered his career, he became more and more complacent and casual about anything spiritual. He was a "good" person but spiritually indifferent. Bruce's spiritual roots were not his own. He never recovered spiritually, continuing in spiritual indifference with a religious facade. His children, in turn, were not even believers.

First, let's concentrate on Christian parents building spiritual independence into their young adults who are believers.

Recall part of our overall parenting goal from chapter 1. Our goal is "that they grow into mature, independent, godly adults . . . who are emotionally and spiritually strong." What does it mean to be spiritually strong? We believe it means that the spiritual beliefs they have been taught become their own convictions, founded soundly upon Scripture, and that these convictions are demonstrated in practical ways in their daily lives.

Regardless of the strength and soundness of their spiritual teaching, experience, and background, doubts and questions will always emerge in the mind of a teenager. They may never verbalize their doubts, but they are present. They question almost everything they were taught and attempt to come up with their own answers.

In this process young adults emerge in their early twenties with a set of beliefs and values distinctly their own. They may abandon faith for a time or their faith may grow deeper. In this period, no amount of external control will guide their minds. They may conform to the external trappings of church or religious life while trying to validate belief with experience using their particular forms of proof.

They will especially begin to question the "do's and don'ts" of their parents and church. All of this investigation provides a fertile ground for conflict.

Drinking, movies of various ratings, music, pornography, videos, dancing, sex, dating, and drugs all emerge as issues for decisions. But they are really surface (though possibly dangerous) issues; external actions that do not necessarily affect deep spiritual beliefs. Certainly, parents wish to affect (even control, at times) some of their actions to protect them. But the deepest goal is to help them develop spiritual roots that will guide their external decisions.

A young adult will inevitably be plagued with certain questions, such as:

- Does God really exist?
- Is the Bible really true?
- Is Jesus Christ the only way to salvation?
- Do I need to believe all of the Bible?
- Are nonChristians really lost?

In addition they will question many of their parental and church values such as baptism, church attendance, specific doctrines, and specific prohibitions.

To hear these questions verbalized can easily disturb parents. We maintain that *not* hearing them should disturb us even more because young adults surely consider these questions. They are seeking the answers somewhere. We may not be able to answer them fully, but we must remember that they don't expect rote answers. They want to talk and reason.

Listen to them. Direct them to resources that may help them. Don't communicate shock or question their sincerity or ridicule them. Let them struggle through. Let them teach you as they discover. We may have accepted certain forms as the Christian norm without ever validating them scripturally. Encourage them to keep examining the Scriptures. Don't expect them to raise a question on Thursday and then spend the next four weeks engrossed in a deep study of the issue! They will bring it up, think on it a bit, and set it back in their memory to resurrect it a few weeks or months later when it bothers them again.

The way a young adult develops his or her beliefs and values often follows a pattern. First there is the *recognition* of the issue. Next there is the *rejection* or partial rejection of the parents' belief or value. Then there is a time of *re-evaluation*. Finally there is *rekindling* of belief or *alteration* of belief. This process takes time—often years. We cannot expect or demand quick resolution. The difficulty of this period is living with the tension of their unresolved issues of belief. As much as we would like them to quickly and decisively adopt our beliefs, in reality such an adoption would most likely produce anemic, stillborn faith—more form than reality.

In helping our young adults become spiritually independent, what are the basic concepts and goals we should strive to implant in their thinking?

1. *Their spiritual beliefs must truly be their own*, not ours.

They must know that we are committed to their personal quest for a relationship with God. They know we do not want them to abandon our beliefs and that knowledge is pressure enough. Personal ownership is imperative.

2. *We must encourage them to search the Scriptures for themselves.* We want them to have confidence that the Bible is the source of all their beliefs and conduct (Acts 17:11). We need to set this pattern and example before them in our own lives.

3. *We want to encourage them to search out answers for themselves* rather than just following someone else's doctrine or conduct. Encourage them to wrestle with the hard questions. This can be frightening since it may raise questions we have not even thought of. But are we afraid to turn them loose with the Bible? We can confidently expect that God will provide them with answers from His Word.

4. *Help them to set a pattern of a daily time spent with God* in reading the Scripture and praying. Encourage this regardless of their feelings, struggles, or questions.

5. *Impress upon them the necessity to always seek out the fellowship of other believers,* especially in a small-group context in addition to some form of corporate worship. During their college years encourage them to find a church that offers a group with on-campus support, or to seek out a group like The Navigators, Campus Crusade for Christ, Inter-Varsity Christian Fellowship, or some other Christian campus group.

6. *Help them to pray for guidance* in each issue of their lives. They can pray even when they are struggling (Matthew 7:7-8).

In this period of their lives, your personal example will speak far more loudly than any words or arguments. How are you doing in these six areas?

You may agree that these are admirable goals, but you

may ask how one builds them into a young adult's life. First, notice the many areas of normal conflict that are not in that list. Young adulthood is a time of sorting out the essentials and nonessentials of belief. Many of the nonessentials (church attendance, conformity to certain standards) may make people feel good but have little relationship to the young adult's deepening spiritual roots.

Second, this is a period when others will likely have a deeper spiritual influence in their lives than we will. Each of our children has had a mature confidant in their lives at this age. (See chapter 9.) Much of their sharing, confiding, questions, and struggles surfaced in that relationship. So pray for a "spiritually significant other" in their lives. Often he or she will be older than your young adult. Never resent or be jealous of him or her. Welcome this person with gratitude for his or her important influence.

Third, avoid a stifling legalism in your counsel. Share your counsel along with your feelings and fears, but let them know the choices are theirs to make. Are there any rules? Certainly, but in the context of protection and practical living, not spiritual belief. More will be said on this later.

Finally, learn to discuss spiritual issues in a nonthreatening, nonargumentative manner. This calls for a radical change from control and coaching to counsel and caring. In this arena, arguments won do not count. Your "I don't know" or "You may be right" could be the most fertile ground for opening up genuine spiritual communication. Treat them as you would your neighbor or friends, not your child.

Our most potent ally is *prayer*. There is no substitute. God listens when our young adults don't. Their spiritual response may be years in coming. Our confidence for them is in God, not our efforts or desires. We care and love deeply through prayer.

Emotional Independence

A young adult can leave home and be financially independent and yet be emotionally dependent on home and parents. Emotional bondage to parents places a young adult in a most unhealthy state. Certainly, emotional ties should exist, but not emotional bondage. Parents can create this emotional servitude either by withholding the encouragement and commendation young adults need to strike out on their own, or by forcing continued allegiance instead of independence.

Beth was the middle of three daughters. Her insecure mother demanded perfection from her girls, feeling her own worth was tied to her daughters' performance in life. Beth's older sister received outstanding grades in school, graduated from a prestigious college, and secured a high-paying job in scientific research. The younger sister won a few teen beauty contests. The mother puts notices in the church bulletin about the older sister's awards for research and keeps the younger sister's contest photos in the living room.

Beth could never find a distinguishing quality to capture her mother's attention. Today at twenty-eight she is a decent, contributing human being, but she still longs for her mother's recognition. She lives several hundred miles from home but calls her mother once or twice a week. Instead of the personal interest she hopes her mother will show, she listens instead to a recital of her sisters' achievements.

Beth's husband and friends can't understand why she doesn't dismiss her mother as a selfish, uncaring woman, but Beth insists that she keeps the contact frequent out of respect and affection for her mother.

Unknowingly and often without intent we as parents can foster an emotional dependence that cripples our children for life. Psychologists and psychiatrists often deal with a person's past emotional relationship with parents. Thousands of people pour out their needs in frequent therapy sessions. We do not presume to solve all those issues in this short section. But we do wish to identify a few specific points upon which parents can act to help their young adults become emotionally independent.

Emotionally healthy parents want to see their children develop strong, stable emotions that permit them to function well in a world of their own. But all parents possess blind spots.

Let's look at some ways to *keep* a young person dependent. We will state the issues in the negative since most of us can see them more clearly than in their positive counterparts. Thus, if you want to keep your children emotionally dependent upon you:

1. Express to them that you do not *trust* them to make good decisions. Have them check everything through with you.
2. Make them *feel guilty* as they leave home and whenever they make decisions that don't please you. Be sure they know they're not meeting your emotional needs.
3. Make them realize that they must *win your approval* in everything they do. Keep your acceptance of them conditional on how you view them and their activities.
4. Discourage deep friendships outside the family. Keep them *chained to family* dependency.
5. Set high expectations of them and *withhold commendation* if your expectations are not met.
6. Keep them feeling that they are *responsible to you* no matter what their age.

Each of these statements demonstrates the strand of a cord that builds emotional bondage or dependence. We need to consciously avoid actions that breed dependence. The quality of our future relationship to our young adults depends on rebuilding the basis of our emotional ties—both in our minds and theirs.

Our past patterns may have so strongly encouraged dependence that we may need to verbally express to our son or daughter our change in thinking, admitting how difficult it will be for us to adjust. In some ways this will grant them an emotional release.

But let's not place all the responsibility on the parents. Some young adults cling to their parents far beyond a healthy stage. They resist making decisions. They delay leaving home. They rely on parents when they could be independent.

Some young people depend on parents out of insecurity, fear, indolence, or habit. Without parental nudging, they may continue that way for years. There are some steps parents can take to urge their children to practice emotional independence:

1. *Refuse to make decisions for them.* Encourage them to think through necessary decisions. Ask questions that will guide their thinking. Pray with them about their decisions. Affirm any initiative they take in decision making.

2. *Encourage other relationships.* As they build strong relationships with peers and others outside the family, their need for emotional dependence on parents will dwindle.

3. *Let them fail.* Parents who always step in to bind up emotional wounds foster dependence. If young adults lose a girlfriend, get fired from a job, or run out of money, sympathize with them but don't always rescue them.

4. *Force independence when necessary.* Insist they find answers and solve problems. In the short term it's painful for parents and young adults. But ultimately everyone benefits. We may need to use the "foot illustration"—the proverbial kick in the pants—to get them to move on in life.

One young man, married for a year, spoke to us with deep frustration etching his face. "My wife's folks have four daughters. We all live within a mile of her folks' place. They insist everybody come to their house every day for at least a little while. We can't have a life of our own because we're always running over there. My wife doesn't want to hurt their feelings by saying no, because her sisters and their husbands and kids all go, but I've about had it." A distinct example of emotional overkill.

Another set of parents we know took an opposite approach. Their daughter Betty had dreamed of becoming a nurse. After graduation, she left her small town and moved a hundred miles away to a large city to train in a metropolitan hospital. After two weeks of desperate homesickness, she climbed on a bus, went home, and declared she would get a job clerking at the hardware store. "I can't stand it there," she wailed. "I'm too homesick."

Her parents firmly put her back in the car and returned her to the hospital. That time she lasted three weeks. Her parents repeated the process. Twice more in the first year they lovingly but insistently returned her to nursing school. She is today an excellent nursing supervisor in a large hospital with a strong respect for her parents' insistence on her independence.

Next to a strong spiritual walk with God, our young adults need emotional independence—a confidence that they can cope on their own. They need to know we're available, but they also need to have confidence that whatever storms of life hit them, they can with God's help survive.

Functional Independence

Every young adult needs to be functionally prepared to live independently. A number of years ago when we led a ministry with college students, the young men in the ministry would occasionally ask me to mend some item or another of clothing on my sewing machine. One day a young student came to the house and said, "Would you mind if I *used* your sewing machine?" That question alerted my thinking to the value of practical preparation for independent living.

When our young adults assume independent living, can they feed, clothe, and house themselves, living within their means? Although ideally they assimilate these skills over a period of years, we can condense and teach the rudiments of functional living in a very short period of time—providing they are *willing* to accept help.

Our society lives at such a high-pitched speed that parents often perform routine tasks of living for young adults rather than taking the time to teach them, assuming that they will absorb the knowledge somehow.

Again, when we were in close contact with students, we were planning a group function once. Several college students offered to make cookies for refreshments, but only half of them had ever baked a cookie before. Now, cookie-baking isn't essential to independent living, but this did indicate a lack of functional experience. The availability of fast foods has taken its toll on cooking skills.

Recently, while waiting in line for lunch in a fast-food restaurant, our youngest daughter and I were approached by a poll taker asking about the use of fast-food restaurants. After we answered several questions, I asked her how often most people used a fast-food restaurant. She answered, "Three or more times per week." An interesting commentary on America's eating habits.

By the time teens leave for college, or take an apartment, or even if they remain at home and work—at any time during and after high school—they should be able to do the following:

1. Select, purchase, and care for all of their clothes. This includes knowledge of fabrics, styles, and costs.

2. Understand basic nutrition and simple meal preparation. Many young adults cannot name the four basic food groups and why they are important for basic health.

3. Maintain a car (even if they do not personally own one), perform simple repairs, change a tire, *keep it clean*, read a road map, and fill the gas tank.

4. Understand insurance. This is important during young adulthood when they are especially vulnerable. They need a basic knowledge of the reasons for and rates behind auto, health, and life insurance.

5. Exercise financial responsibility. This skill is so basic that we must spend extra time discussing it. Functional independence achieved at home will not benefit young adults unless they know how to pay for it. Financial competence takes years to achieve, but practice and guidance under a parent's experienced eye may help prevent major mistakes.

We need to realize and accept that our sons and daughters will initially need to adjust to a lower standard of living than they have enjoyed at home. Ultimately they may make far more money than we do, but their power as a wage earner will likely develop slowly.

In her book *The Postponed Generation* Susan Littwin comments on the attitude of many young people in the coming-of-age generation when she says, "They set great store by having a stylish place to live. This is not a generation of pioneers. They are just kids with a high sense of *entitlement* and a not so high sense of reality"[1] (italics ours).

We perform a distinct favor for our young adults when we allow them to struggle and succeed, try and triumph, attempt and accomplish. They will fail along the way, as we did, but they will have a heightened awareness of what *they* can do.

One of our daughters disliked having to ask us for money during her high school years, and yet her needs seemed to be many. We talked the situation over with her and arrived at a plan. We gave her a sum from the household budget each month. With that money she was expected to pay for all her needs. The only expenses we covered were room and board and any charges associated with her church youth activities, such as weekend retreats.

The amount of her allowance was less than she realistically needed. So she found jobs like housecleaning and baby-sitting to cover her needs and perhaps pay for an occasional luxury. She made mistakes but she learned too. One month she was tempted by a beautiful pair of leather boots, and for the next month she had only socks with holes to put in the boots. We would have dearly loved to have bought her many pairs of socks, but that would have destroyed her confidence in her own beginning budgeting ability. Ultimately she developed good financial habits, learning through trial and error.

Parents can give the most financial help through the following:

1. *Help your teens establish and keep a budget.* Emphasize saving and if they don't have an established savings account, help them open one. Emphasize giving, remembering that generosity is much more a matter of attitude than legalistic ritual. Suggest giving options if they have trouble deciding where to give—church, specific missionaries, family relief, or orphan support.

2. *Help them open and maintain a checking account.* We made the mistake of waiting until our son and daughters were nearly ready for independent living before helping them open their personal accounts. One daughter later told us that she followed a pattern she learned from a classmate. When her account became hopelessly muddled, she merely

closed it and opened another at a bank down the street. Another daughter told us, "I don't want to bother with reconciling my checking account. I can just call the bank and ask them how much money I have." If we had helped them establish their accounts earlier, they could have avoided some of their banking snafus.

Credit cards are a debatable issue. Some parents prefer to let their children use a family card with a specific spending limit. This tests the responsibility and integrity of the young adult. Other parents recommend an individual account that offers the young person a chance to develop stable, trustworthy habits. We suggest that no young adult use a credit card unless the amount is paid in full on a monthly basis.

CONCLUSIONS

What a challenge it is to help our young adults enter independence spiritually, emotionally, and functionally. Although we coach and counsel, they ultimately will make their own decisions. Our part is to cover them with caring and prayer and trust God to guide their steps.

4

Coaching
Decision Making

Recently we had dinner in our home with a visitor from Nigeria, Africa. During the conversation we asked him what he noticed was different about our culture from his. He thought for a moment and then said, "In my country my father feels the freedom, indeed, the responsibility, to monitor my decisions, and to tell me when I am making mistakes. Although I am nearly forty years old, he still guides my decisions and will do so as long as he lives."

He paused, and then added, "I notice that doesn't happen here."

How right he is! In our society most decision-making responsibility has passed to the individual by the time he or she is eligible to vote. Many times parents would like to direct their young adults' lives, but it just doesn't happen that way.

Although parents can't *make* decisions for their offspring, they can continue to influence and counsel if they involve themselves in the right way.

All parents want to see their maturing sons and daughters make wise choices and godly decisions that will lead them into productive, happy lives. But many parents stand suffering on the sidelines while their offspring make irresponsible or disastrous decisions.

Some decisions lead to difficult but necessary lessons. At age nineteen Doug bought a new car without consulting his parents or anyone else. In his naiveté he borrowed money from a loan shark who charged an exorbitant rate of interest. The pleasure of owning a new car wore off long before that loan was paid. His parents let him bear the financial burden, knowing he would learn from the experience. And so he did. Never again has he taken out a car loan. He saves and then pays cash for any car he buys.

That decision brought temporary setbacks, but parents' deepest grief comes when they see poor decisions that result in lifelong tragedy and waste.

Jake and Lynn's daughter, Sue, entered a distant college at age seventeen. She had been sheltered and protected during her growing years, coddled in a loving Christian home and educated in a small Christian school. The large university atmosphere stunned her—the drug scene, the ridicule of spiritual values, the immorality in the dormitories. Lonely and isolated at first, she gradually began to adopt the thinking and activities of her classmates.

By the end of her freshman year she smoked marijuana daily, was failing in three of her four classes, and was four months pregnant.

Sue left school and returned to her parents' home. Amid many tears Jake and Lynn discussed with her what course of action to follow. She decided to give birth and place the child with a Christian adoption agency.

But she suffered severe guilt and depression and required two years of periodic hospitalization and counseling before finally recovering. Although Sue is married now, Jake and Lynn still occasionally see a faraway look in her eyes and know that she's remembering the child lost to her by decisions that nearly destroyed her life.

Imagine Adam and Eve's anguish when they discovered Cain's decision to murder his brother Abel (Genesis 4), or King David's sorrow as he fled from Jerusalem, hounded from the throne by the traitorous decision of his son Absalom (2 Samuel 15).

But other biblical parents experienced the joy of seeing the next generation make wise decisions with positive, lasting effects. Eunice and Lois watched young Timothy choose to follow the Apostle Paul and devote his life to the first-century Church (2 Timothy 1:5). And Hannah, from a distance, watched Samuel grow and mature making decisions that influenced and guided a nation (1 Samuel 1).

The story of Daniel gives us an encouraging example. Although ripped away from his family and culture while still a youth, he stood firm in his decisions to honor God. Even without parental guidance and influence, he chose to follow a righteous path. He continued worshiping the living God. He refused the pleasures of the flesh in the king's palace, and he led other young Hebrew men in the same path.

We can pray for similar commitment and courage for our young adults.

Parents need to be prepared to accept decisions made by their young adults, to influence where possible, and to let them live with the consequences. We as parents can best prepare for this important task by being firmly established in our own walk of faith, and by having confidence that God will work His perfect plan for our young adults.

A daily time of reading God's Word and praying will stabilize us during even the most trying situations. We may face times when only God's comfort will see us through the upheaval and catastrophe brought about by our young adults' poor decisions. Even the caring concern of loving friends can't match the comfort of a close relationship with

God. Only faith in God and His love will bring parents through those times.

HOW YOUNG ADULTS MAKE DECISIONS

Several factors affect the way young adults make decisions.

1. *Parental example.* As our young adults observe the way we make decisions they will be profoundly affected. Admitting and evaluating our mistakes can help them avoid similar problems. Seeing our good patterns can help them learn to make good decisions. The environment in which we raise our children will affect their ability to follow our example when they are grown.

Are we impetuous or deliberate in our approach to major decisions? Do we make choices that are legal but not ethical? Do our young adults see and hear us praying about our decisions? Are the decisions we make about our time, money, and personal energy selfish or generous? In all of these areas our style and example will influence our sons and daughters.

2. *Personality and intellect.* Each person makes decisions based on his or her unique individuality, personality, and style of thinking. All these characteristics are God-ordained and serve to influence the direction and strength of personal decisions. These traits appear in childhood and rarely change; rather, they strengthen during the teen years. As our children mature into adults some of the negative aspects will be modified or canceled.

3. *Spiritual vitality.* Daily communion with God and prayer about their decisions will help young adults make mature decisions in all areas of life. Parents can encourage growth in this area both by personal example and by offering to participate in a time of prayer and spiritual sharing with their sons and daughters. Encourage them toward environ-

ments where these values are stimulated.

4. Education and training. A young adult who has been foolish in past decisions may learn new approaches from both academic and spiritual training. Although basic personalities remain the same for a lifetime, training can influence the way we respond to life's circumstances. For instance, a girl who had a reputation for flighty, impetuous behavior trained as a paramedic. Much to the surprise of her family and friends she is now capable and calm in even the most disastrous medical emergencies.

5. Peer and societal influence. This strong tug on young adults influences many of their decisions: what movies to see, what cars to buy, what careers to enter, ways to date, mates to choose, and churches to attend.

The clout that society wields on our young adults cannot be underestimated. We delude ourselves if we think that our example and counsel exert the most dominance in our young adults' decision making. The power of the media and the pressure from peers push them daily to make choices—not always ungodly or unwise but often against our personal wishes.

6. Styles of thinking. All of the previous factors influence our offspring, as well as ourselves, in the way decisions are made. But another heavily contributing factor is the way we think. One of the greatest sources of misunderstanding between parents and young adults comes when we fail to understand the thinking processes of one another. We have heard many comments to verify this fact.

From parents:

"I don't understand that kid. Twenty-one years old and still trying to decide on a college major. He'll be forty before he finally decides what he wants to do. If he thinks I'll support him in college that long, he can think again!" "She's absolutely the most stubborn girl in the world. When she

makes up her mind, it's useless to try to reason with her."
"He has the wildest ideas! Why can't he settle down and live a normal life like everybody else?"

And from the young adults:

"My dad can't see beyond the end of his nose. He absolutely refuses to listen to another point of view." "Mom is forty-eight, but you'd never know it by the decisions she makes. She can't ever make up her mind, and if she does, she's likely to change it the next day." "My folks are always so logical about everything. Why can't they loosen up and enjoy life?"

Obviously, misunderstandings abound between parents and maturing adults. Individual thinking styles contribute significantly to these disagreements and rifts. Because we think differently based on our intellect, backgrounds, personalities, and environments, we are headed for conflict unless we are able to grasp the thinking style of family members. Different styles of thinking aren't right or wrong, they just are. We discern these differences by noticing some of the colloquial expressions that have evolved in our language: scatterbrained, egghead, highbrow, dumbbell, and dizzy dame.

It is useless to criticize another person for his or her method of thinking. With effort, a person can change his or her approach somewhat, but why? A much better answer is to discern the way our young adults and other family members think and then get in step with their ideas. That doesn't mean we accept stupidity or foolishness on their part, but that we respond to differences of opinion with understanding. We don't always have to agree, but we can understand why they chose their point of view.

What are some styles of thinking? Some detailed scientific studies have been done in this area, but for our purposes, we will be simple.

Analytical thinkers. These people see all sides of a problem, weigh the possibilities against each other, and reach a decision. They have a realistic view of current circumstances as well as a view of future results of present decisions.

Intuitive thinkers. They have little regard for heavy analysis but respond because "it *feels* right." Intuitive thinkers quickly respond with sensitivity to the joys and trials of others. But they may make decisions on the emotion of the moment, disregarding the long-term results of those decisions.

Creative thinkers. Their ideas are far-out and ahead of the majority of the crowd. They love new, imaginative, innovative ways of approaching life. Their minds are fertile and active. They often generate ten ideas to every one that can be effectively implemented, but that doesn't seem to discourage the flow of ideas. They discard the other nine and keep right on thinking.

Logical thinkers. These folks appreciate a step-by-step progression from the onset of a question or a problem to the finish. No leaping from one possibility to another. They reflect and deliberate carefully before deciding, speaking, and acting. Logical thinkers balance their checkbooks, drive within the speed limit, and make great organizers.

Visionary thinkers. These are the conquerors, the inventors, the originators in all fields of endeavor. They are rarely concerned with mundane details but see lofty possibilities for themselves and others. Usually they are able motivators and influencers, and they leave the implementation to the analytical and logical thinkers.

And of course there are many combinations of the above styles of thinking. When we blend those styles of thinking with personality traits—steady, impetuous, thoughtful, stubborn, rebellious, considerate, compliant, hostile, pleasant—we have the large task before us of understanding and appreciating one another.

It's easy to dismiss another person's thinking style as frivolous, stubborn, illogical, or bizarre simply because we don't think that way ourselves. Granted, some thinking and decisions do fall into those categories, but often it's just *different*. God has uniquely created each one of us to make a contribution to the family, the Body of Christ, and the world. That uniqueness extends to our thinking styles and our decision making.

Once we realize the effect varying thinking styles will have on decision making, we can consider how we want to influence our young adults. We want to influence only those decisions that will have a lifetime effect. Again, remember, "Don't sweat the small stuff."

In what areas will our young adults be making lifechanging choices: Commitment to Christ? Moral and ethical dilemmas? Relationships? Education? Marriage? Career?

If these choices were presented one at a time, in logical order, how easy it would be. But life isn't like that. Circumstances force decisions when young adults aren't prepared for them or even expecting them.

If we have developed and maintained a strong enough relationship with our offspring, we will have an opportunity to counsel and guide them through some potentially rough periods. Again, always keep in mind that they may choose to exclude us completely, both from knowledge of the problem and from counseling them.

That is the hardest parental position to be in. We want to help, we want to counsel and pray with them, but we're excluded. That makes consistent, intensive prayer for them all the more important, as we don't always know what they are experiencing.

When one of our daughters was a college student, she told us of a fellow student, a young man, whose girlfriend got pregnant. Both were students, nineteen years old, and financially dependent on their parents. Neither considered telling their parents or drawing them into the process.

For three weeks they talked about the problem from every angle, with the young man pleading with her not to kill his child. But desperate and feeling the urgency to decide, the young woman had an abortion. Both students keenly regretted the loss of the child, but didn't know what else to do. Their parents never knew of the lost grandchild, or of the desperation their teenagers experienced.

How fortunate are those parents whose young adults will ask them for specific counsel and help. In most cases we will need to coach and counsel more subtly. Blasting into a young adult's life guarantees resistance and conflict. Wisdom, sensitivity, and prayer pave the way to interaction.

GOALS OF PARENTAL COACHING

Our goals in coaching decisions should help our sons and daughters see these two important points:

1. *Predict and understand the future consequences of their decisions.* This is a very difficult concept for most young people to grasp. Life seems to stretch long and unending before them. They feel invincible. They have, in the past, been protected from the full consequences of foolish decisions by parental intervention and societal tolerance.

Even young people who trust God have difficulty realizing the potential dangers and disasters that result from poor decisions. They haven't yet had to review the disaster of a decision that led to years of regret. They know intellectually that God forgives, but they haven't had to live with the scars.

All decisions have parameters and consequences. If a teenager chooses to drink in excess, he or she will get drunk, perhaps do stupid—even criminal—things, and suffer a hangover the next day. Choices always produce consequences.

We can help them see that failure to study leads to a failing grade, drinking and then driving results in wrecks, overdrawing a bank account leads to monetary penalties, spiritual indifference means spiritual poverty.

2. *Learn to sacrifice present pleasures for future fulfillment.* This is a hard one for young people. They live very much in the here and now, and focus on excitement, fun, happiness, activity, and current relationships. Getting caught up in the emotion of the moment, many teens fail to consider the long-term results of present decisions.

We can determine if our young adults are recognizing the need to sacrifice present pleasures by some of the choices they make. Would they give up a party to study for a test? Forgo some entertainment to save money for a spring break trip? Sacrifice free time to help a friend in need? Avoid sex now to enter marriage as a virgin? Work at a job to help pay for education?

AIDING THE DECISION-MAKING PROCESS

When we are informed of a decision facing our teens, we should *never* offer an immediate opinion. Even if the choice seems obvious, direct advice isn't a helpful approach. In the first place, it will probably be rejected, not so much for content as for the way it was offered. Secondly, direct advice doesn't help the teenager develop the thinking processes necessary for prudent decisions.

One of our young adults called one day from the college dormitory and said, "Hey, Mom, can I have $550?" Managing to restrain my immediate response—No!—I listened to the explanation that there was an irresistible motorcycle for sale that would be *so* much better for transportation than a bicycle. After delaying an immediate answer, we talked again the next day and the initial enthusiasm had worn off. If I had been immediately negative—as I am often inclined to be— conflict and resentment would have been the result.

If we can approach our young adults with a sense of concern, interest, and understanding, we might be allowed to interact with them. Nonthreatening questions help to open a dialogue, like, "I'm interested in hearing your ideas about that. Could you tell me what you're thinking at this point?" It's also important to be honest in our questioning. If we say we're interested, we must *be* interested. Our offspring can detect hypocrisy more quickly than we would care to admit. Then let's *listen* with a goal of *understanding*.

Understanding will require patience, sensitivity, time, and help from the Lord. Parents have had a lifetime to determine how their maturing children think, but total comprehension is never complete. They are progressing and evolving in their approach to life, and so are we. God hasn't completed His work in any of us, and change is inevitable.

Perhaps they are facing a problem or decision that has several possible good answers. One of our teenagers was accepted at three colleges and faced a major task of choosing the right one for her. She *wanted* our input, perhaps even wanted us to relieve her of the necessity to decide, but after much discussion, she finally made her own choice. Not always, however, do our young adults welcome our input, and in those cases we must be prepared to stand on the sidelines and enter the process only when we are invited by them.

Sometimes we can establish artificial parameters to guide right decisions. We can withhold funding for an improper choice of college. We can refuse to loan our car to a reckless driver. We can insist on professional counseling for a troubled young adult in exchange for a home to live in or support money.

Most of the time, though, decisions cannot, indeed should not, be artificially controlled. Whenever the communication allows it, parents and teens can dialogue on the consequences of choices, allowing the young adults to *discover* for themselves the results of their decisions.

Encourage them to avoid impetuous decisions. A good friend of ours says, "There are good decisions, and there are fast decisions, but there are no good, fast decisions." Even if they allow a night to pass, or an hour, they may view the situation in a different light.

We can help when we counsel our young adults as we would share advice and counsel with any other adult—nondirective, but wise, practical, and beneficial.

Here are some specific ideas on training and coaching in the area of decision making:

1. Analyze your own decision-making style, bias, and history.
2. Help young adults determine what kind of thinker they are.
3. Involve them in the decision-making process.
4. Let them fail. You can't always rescue them.
5. When you become aware of a decision in process, listen, question, rarely give directive advice, cooperate with their style of thinking, encourage them to wait, encourage them to seek counsel from other godly adults.
6. Help them analyze past decisions for the positive and negative aspects of those decisions.
7. Pray for wisdom for them.
8. Support them once the decision has been made.

What should we avoid as we seek to assist our sons and daughters with their decisions?

1. Never say "I told you so" when they blunder. Sometimes we will be strongly tempted to do so, but it always ruins future communication.
2. Avoid criticism. If the decision has been translated into action, it's too late.
3. Nagging, overemphasis, and drawn-out advice will not win a hearing. Counsel with few words.
4. Avoid conflict if possible. It's a sure sign of defeat in giving counsel.
5. Don't get angry if your counsel isn't followed. Allow circumstances to counsel your young adult.

CONCLUSIONS

Every young adult faces critical decisions that will set the course of his or her lifetime. Parents can get behind those decisions with prayer, a godly personal example, understanding, and counsel. Remember, too, that someday we will be dependent on their counsel and help in our decisions. The training and influence we give them now will benefit them and us in those days to come.

5

Building Career Preparation

We ask small children, "What do you want to be when you grow up?"

"A fireman."

"A pilot."

"An astronaut."

"A mother."

Then during the early teens the answers change.

Almost every adult asks young people in their late teens, "What are you planning to do?" The question becomes so commonplace and irritating to most young adults that they soon come up with a standard, acceptable answer: "Go to college and study business"—or engineering, or medicine, or some other good-sounding answer. Or they might say, "Get training to become a paramedic"—or a mechanic, or a secretary, or a computer operator.

The question produces anxiety, because most young adults don't know what they want to do. Or what they really want to do sounds so silly they don't dare mention it. Many would like to say to those prying adults, "I'd like to goof off, travel to the beaches, get a good tan, go to college part-time, and have my parents support me for a few more years!" But they don't say that because it's not polite or acceptable. They give, instead, fine-sounding goals for their careers and futures. But underneath their confident statements about the future lies an anxious pressure to perform and succeed—to *be someone.*

Most young adults today discover that at age eighteen, or even twenty-two, they do not possess a clear picture of what they want to do with their lives and careers, whereas most of us, their parents, set out into adult life with a clear idea of what we would become.

EXPECTATIONS AND REALITIES

For those of us in our forties and fifties, our father had one career and two jobs. We ourselves have two careers and three to five jobs. Our children will have three to five careers and five to ten jobs. These are sobering statistics.

Part of the cause lies in the rapidly changing technology and job market of our age. We live in a different world than our parents did. We may realize it even more if we have recently been without a job or have had to change career fields. Then we discover that much of our training and many of our skills are obsolete.

Other factors seem to be endemic to this generation. Young adults are postponing their life decisions more and more. In her book *The Postponed Generation* Susan Littwin attempts to explain the statement, "Why American Youth Are Growing Up Later." She particularly concentrates on the children of middle-class parents. Littwin reports,

> Studies by the University of Michigan's Institute for Social Research and by the social survey research team of Yankelovich, Skelly, and White show that young Americans feel increasingly goalless and anxious. . . .

The crisis they face is part of their special history. They were raised in the sixties when we were all greening and changing in various ways and—best of all— knew that we could afford to do so and believed that our children would also be able to. If we never told them that life could be tough, it was because we had forgotten it ourselves.[1]

. . . it would turn out that the expectations they grew up with weren't going to work—at least not in reality. But they lived on in fantasy and since the fantasies were so much nicer, it was reality that had to go. . . . They lament that so many jobs are in the city rather than up in the mountains where the air is cleaner. Or they leave entry-level jobs because the company did not implement their ideas immediately.

It is hard enough to establish an adult identity, even in the best of times. But to do it with such a jarring conflict between expectation and reality is a stunning task. What many of today's twenty- to thirty-year-olds have elected to do is continue the identity search while avoiding reality, and that makes it exceedingly slow work.[2]

Littwin's analysis paints a bleak picture of this generation. Yet in young adult after young adult, and from parent after parent, the generalizations are confirmed. You may be blessed with a young adult who is very self-directed and goal-oriented. Be grateful, for in many areas he or she is the exception rather than the rule.

We can deplore our society, but that does not change it. Our young adults have grown up in that society and bear its marks as surely as we bear the marks of World War II and the post-war society. Thus, we must try to understand their environment, motivations, and pressures, which are unique to them and their generation.

We must first realize that they will likely *not* have a clear idea of their career futures. In fact, they may change directions several times. A father told us, "My daughter is twenty-one. She's been in college for two separate semesters and has already held seven jobs. She is rootless and undirected, and it doesn't seem to bother her a bit, but it sure bothers me."

A second realization is that our position is only to *coach* and *counsel*, never to control. Their future must be theirs alone.

We want our young adults to have a hierarchy of concerns as they face the future. Here is a hierarchy that parents desire:

- Spiritual
- Physical
- Emotional/Psychological
- Future (job, marriage, etc.)

In practice, however, the spiritual often takes a lower position. In this hierarchy, a parent's most pressing concerns center on the current problem. For instance, serious physical illness take precedence in our minds over all other problems. When basic spiritual, physical, and emotional issues are relatively secure, our focus centers on our young adults' future.

For each of our daughters, the hierarchical lineup of concerns for her future resembled the following:

Will she be married?
    To whom?
    What will her husband do?
What skills for employment will she have?
    What education will she need?
    How much training is required?

For a son, the concerns line up differently:

> What job will he pursue?
>> What education will he need?
>> How much training is required?
> Will he be married?
>> To whom?
>> What is her background?

Whatever one thinks of the role of men and women in the current debate over equal rights, we believe this represents the predominant parental focus. We are products of our upbringing and environment. In this chapter we will address the career concept. Marriage is treated in chapter 6.

The sixteen-to-twenty-two-year age bracket is one of the most determinative times for career direction. The environment where young adults prepare for careers will often be the environment where they will meet and marry their future mate. If they bum around bars, they will probably marry someone who does the same. If they attend college, they are likely to meet and fall in love with another college student. If they are active in church circles, they will probably meet someone there. Many parents want their young adults to meet someone who has a high drive-level and a good potential for earning a high income. But that may not be what their young adults need, or what is God's best for them.

There are three primary ways to enter a career path: through university education; by attending a junior or community college or technical training institute; or through direct work experience.

Which is preferable? There is no preference. The direction for your young adult depends upon many factors. You as a parent may have strong feelings or preferences. If you went to college, you may insist your son or daughter do so as well. If you are a technician or craftsman, you may want your young adult to follow that path. Or you may want him or her to avoid some of your hard times and, therefore, encourage a different path. But all that is *your* thinking.

What about your young adult's hopes and dreams? He or she must live in his or her future. Your task is to help your young adult discover and choose what fits him or her best.

We realize that every person must have some kind of vocation to live in society. But your young adult is just coming to that understanding, and full-time work produces anxiety the nearer it comes.

On what basis do we counsel him or her? The keys to choosing a viable career path are the following:

- *Natural abilities*—academics, motivation, manual dexterity, technical and mechanical skill, artistic skill, people skills, leadership.
- *Spiritual abilities*—closely related to natural abilities, the *supernatural* gifting that God's Spirit activates in the lives of Christians in tune with Him.
- *Personal interests*—hobbies, recreational interests, use of spare time, high school classes.
- *Natural intellect or intelligence*—scholastic aptitude tests, school grades, reasoning ability.
- *Motivational patterns*—what turns them on, the driving forces of life, personal stimulus.
- *Opportunity*—finances, job offers, contacts.

Each of these factors will give some direction. Our dilemma is that many young adults mature late, so these factors do not become apparent until then, or if these factors are apparent early, our young adults may refuse to follow through with them. The key is to be patient and wait. They may need some transition time from discovery of interest and talent to practical application.

One young man attended college briefly, then worked for a number of years as a school custodian. Finally he returned to the university, earned a teaching degree, and returned to the school as a teacher. Ironically, he took an initial cut in salary to enter the classroom.

We will divide discussion here into two (rather than three) career paths—university, and a combination of technical school and direct work experience.

THE COLLEGE EXPERIENCE

I have often wondered why I went to a university when no one in my family background had ever done so. Yet very early in high school the idea was implanted and I never doubted that I would. My parents never pushed it—or discouraged it. As God would have it, my academic ability was strong in math and engineering so it was a good choice. But I chose.

Is a university education today all it once was? We think not. There is such a flood of university graduates into the marketplace that a degree no longer guarantees a job at all, especially in the nonspecialized fields. This fact seems to escape parents and young adults alike as they prepare for a career.

The Bureau of Labor Statistics keeps a finger on the occupational pulse of our nation. In its current report it states, "The long-term shift from goods-producing to service-producing employment will continue. By 2000, nearly 4 out of 5 jobs will be industries that provide services—industries such as banking, insurance, health care, education, data processing and management consulting."[3] Such information can prove very helpful for parents and young adults who are discussing future education and career plans.

For young adults drawn to international missions, the right career path is vitally important, for by the year 2000, eighty percent of the countries of the world will be closed to traditional missionaries, and only Christians with practical occupations will be welcomed in those countries.

Thomas J. Moore of the *Chicago Sun-Times* found in extensive research that "There were about twice as many college graduates as there were college-level jobs. And more than 40 percent of these graduates were working at jobs that didn't require a college education. Instead, they were competing with high school graduates and driving job qualifications up."[4]

Almost anyone in the United States can now go to college regardless of Scholastic Aptitude Test (SAT) scores or demonstrated ability. In many ways this is a blessing for those who desire college but whose background is not academically sound. On the other hand, it devalues the premium of a college degree. In fact, a college degree today is about like a high school degree of fifty years ago in terms of exclusiveness and entrance into a job market.

College has been called the "initiation rite for the American middle class"—an expectation of the family, but it can also be an escape from reality, a delay in taking responsibility.

So let's unwrap the glamour of going to a university and bring it into a realistic perspective. We must adjust thinking that tries to push everyone into college. It is no guarantee of either security or career satisfaction.

Let us also remember that a university education is not an end in itself. It is a means to entering the marketplace as well as an environment where a person learns to think more broadly.

We do not mean to be negative about a university education, having pursued it ourselves and having had three of our children attend and graduate, with our last daughter just beginning. But we do want to emphasize that it is *one* option—a good one for motivated young adults at the *right* time.

As indicated earlier, a college degree is a necessity today for many careers. It is also an option for *any* young adult who really wants to attend, regardless of finances. What are the advantages of a university education? It offers

- a significant time of social development,
- expansion of educational and intellectual horizons,
- training for many fields requiring specialized higher education,
- being away from home,
- development of independent living,
- a controlled and measured challenge to personal achievement.

Here are some factors to consider as you coach and counsel young adults regarding a college education:

- High school grades should be above 2.75 (out of 4.0) and preferably about 3.0;
- Scholastic Aptitude Test (SAT) or A College Testing (ACT) scores should be in the upper fiftieth percentile;
- Motivation and desire to go to college should be there; and
- The young adult should show interest in areas for which college preparation is necessary.

Certainly, other factors enter into the decision, but these four are primary, especially for entrance to a four-year university. When they are not met, raise serious questions to your young adult about entering college. If motivation is very strong and the other areas weak, we suggest either waiting a year or building up academic skills in a junior or community college.

Entering and attending a university is the start, but finishing should be the objective. A partial education is scarcely more valuable in the job market than none at all. *Finishing* must be a central goal. One credit away from a degree still means no degree. Being close does not count on a job application. It is good for training in thinking, but of little help in finding a job. Part of the educational experience is demonstrating the ability to finish and reach a goal.

You may wonder why finances were not included in addition to the four factors above. Certainly they are an important factor. However, in today's world of education, such a wide range of options exists for obtaining a college education—student loans, scholarships, financial aid, low-cost junior colleges, work programs, and more. In the United States, a student who really *wants* to attend college can do so, perhaps slowly and not at the most expensive institutions, but it is still possible. Every university and college has a financial aid office that will explain all options to parents and entering students. High school counselors have basic information on how to obtain funds.

Now we will discuss a very touchy aspect of parental involvement in a young adult's education. In many cases, you as the parent pay part or most of the educational costs of a college student, often at a great personal sacrifice. Though the parent's posture in this eighteen-to-twenty-two-year-old period must be one of coaching and counsel with emphasis on counsel, the introduction of the financial element raises the specter of control. Finances raise a conflict-stirring dilemma in the college experience. Should the withdrawal of finances be a threat contingent on some standard of performance? Is that not the ultimate control?

To *not* require responsibility is actually a violation of the young adult's freedom and independence. From high school graduation onward, freedom and independence must be balanced with responsibility. The young adult who chooses to enter the working world directly certainly lives by that code. So must the student. But with the student, the complication is the emotional tie to the provider of funds.

One of the main areas of pressure for a young adult is the success expectations from parents—a performance focus. But that is not the issue here. A parent supporting a college student is, in essence, that student's employer. Every employer insists on a degree of performance or production before the employee is rewarded with a paycheck. The same should follow for a college student. Performance is a prerequisite for support.

There should be agreement on minimum performance measured by grades and number of credit hours taken. We also recommend that the student earn partial support by working, especially during breaks and in the summer.

Let the student set what he or she believes is a minimum standard to continue receiving financial aid. Then negotiate an agreement. Make it clear that his or her "job" is to go to school. We suggest a minimum grade no lower than a B average. Requiring an A average is unrealistic and discouraging for the student. The requirement could be as low as 2.5 (on a 4.0 scale) if the young adult is not highly gifted academically. Or parents may want to adopt a C average for struggling students just as the university does.

If the young adult drops below this agreed-to goal in a given term, find out if there are mitigating circumstances. If so, give him or her another opportunity. Treat it like a business proposition, not as a judgment on him or her as a person.

A final word on college. Do not force your young adult

to go. The decision should rest with him or her. If it is not the young adult's choice, the motivation to work diligently and finish will be low.

ENTERING THE WORK FORCE

Not everyone should go to college, even if qualified to do so. A close friend of ours went to a major university as a freshman. After two months, he concluded that it was a waste of his time. His goal was to be successful financially and he did not see his courses helping him do that. So he quit. He began his own business, developing it over a number of years into a multimillion dollar venture.

He is an exceptional person with unique drive and ability to do whatever he attempts. Others like him find college neither a motivating nor a learning experience. Some young adults should go directly into the work force. It will be a real shock to most. It will force them to grow and cope with "real life" more quickly than those who go to college. Young adults should *not* work toward a four-year degree when any of the following are true:

- They have little motivation.
- Their academic demonstration has been poor.
- Their interests lie in other areas.
- They need more time to "grow up" and mature.
- They do it just to please their parents.

The most compelling reason to enter the work force is to develop a distinct skill or profession that requires experience more than college training. There are many ways to get experience—apprenticeships, training while on the job, or going to specialized classes (welding, secretarial, computer skills, etc.). Just as a college student will likely change majors two or three times, so a young adult in the eighteen-to-twenty-two-year bracket will likely go through several jobs before finding an area where he or she really fits in and finds satisfaction.

It is common for parents to consider helping a young adult go to college. But what about preparing for a career that requires other training? Most parents would consider financing technical or other types of training or learning experiences. Just as you might help seek out a college, help your son or daughter seek out practical training schools or opportunities. You can receive help as you do this from school counselors, other parents, and local reference librarians.

At some point in their first three years out of high school young adults should attend a community or junior college for one year specifically to work on certain skills. These skills will allow them to be more successful in any area of work. They should take courses in reading skills, writing and compositional skills, basic mathematics, and basic computer operation. Each of these areas is mandatory for able functioning in today's society. They are necessary life skills.

PRINCIPLES

Whether eighteen-to-twenty-two-year-old adults go to college or directly enter the workplace, certain values should undergird our counsel and their thinking.

They need to understand the value and need for *hard work*. Both Solomon and the Apostle Paul emphasized this value. Solomon wrote, "The sluggard's craving will be the death of him, because his hands refuse to work" (Proverbs 21:25). And Paul exhorted us with these words: "Whatever you do, work at it with all your heart, as working for the Lord, not for men" (Colossians 3:23).

In a day of ease and leisure, hard work is not always a

value readily adopted by young adults. Yet it is a value that will serve them well all their lives. Privileges and opportunities handed to them may not help them in the long run.

Five Values Young Adults Need

1. They need to learn the value of *perseverance*. M. Scott Peck begins his book *The Road Less Traveled* with the observation, "Life is difficult. This is a great truth, one of the greatest truths. . . . Life is a series of problems. Do we want to moan about them or solve them? Do we want to teach our children to solve them?"[5]

2. He writes on to describe the importance of *discipline*, another aspect of perseverance: "Discipline is the basic set of tools we require to solve life's problems."[6]

The Bible adds a further dimension to the difficulties of life. James encourages us to "consider it pure joy, my brothers, whenever you face trials of many kinds, because you know that the testing of your faith develops perseverance. Perseverance must finish its work so that you may be mature and complete, not lacking anything" (James 1:2-4). Life will always surprise us with problems and difficulties. We all must learn discipline and perseverance that lead to maturity.

3. In the context of employment, *dependability and loyalty* are great assets. In a day when company loyalty is almost a thing of the past, these characteristics will be highly valued. This is how the writer of Proverbs speaks of a reliable person: "Like the coolness of snow at harvest time is a trustworthy messenger to those who send him; he refreshes the spirit of his masters. . . . Like a bad tooth or a lame foot is reliance on the unfaithful in times of trouble" (Proverbs 25:13,19).

4. We want our young adults to be *men and women of their word*. What they pledge they must do. This is the essence of dependability. If they are Christians, it is the

God-honoring thing to do.

They need an unmovable commitment to honesty. In matters of money, information, relationships, and responsibility, honesty has no equal. This value is also losing ground in our society. In *Honesty, Morality, and Conscience*, I wrote, "Honesty, as described in the Bible, is much broader than simply abstaining from lying. . . . Honesty involves an upright way of life and proper thought patterns that result in an honorable lifestyle."[7]

The writer of Proverbs tells us, "Better is the poor who walks in his integrity, than he who is crooked though he be rich" (Proverbs 28:6, NASB).

5. A young adult's insurance for the future is the quality of being *teachable*. The attitude of a learner always gains favor. Pride and ego keep us from learning and growing. Encourage and demonstrate to your young adults that they can learn something from everyone. Every job, menial or managerial, requires learning. A heart to learn is a worthy characteristic not only in God's eyes, but in the eyes of an employer.

The first few chapters of Proverbs often repeat the value of learning—"turning your ear to wisdom and applying your heart to understanding, and if you call out for insight and cry aloud for understanding . . . then you will understand the fear of the LORD" (Proverbs 2:2,3,5). In *The Living Bible* we read an apt paraphrase of Proverbs 12:1: "To learn, you must want to be taught."

We believe these five values to be intrinsic to the building of a sure foundation in the lives of young adults. Whatever direction they choose in pursuing a career, do all you can to first of all model, and then build these five values into the lives of your sons and daughters.

In the midst of this formation every young adult will wrestle with the value of work. Is work a dull necessity or is it a rewarding part of God's plan for life? Since the area of work is treated elsewhere, we refer you to the following books: Jerry and Mary White, *On the Job: Survival or Satisfaction* (Colorado Springs, Colo.: NavPress, 1988); and Doug Sherman and William Hendricks, *Your Work Matters to God* (Colorado Springs, Colo.: NavPress, 1988).

For helping a young adult determine a career direction, we suggest: Arthur Miller and Ralph Mattson, *Finding a Job You Can Love* (Nashville: Thomas Nelson Publishers, 1982); and Richard Bolles, *What Color Is Your Parachute?* (Berkeley, Calif.: Ten Speed Press, 1974).

In this regard, we are not just emphasizing a success-oriented work ethic, but a view of work that comes from God. Our reason for work must go far beyond mere subsistence and survival to the essence of all of life under the purposes of God.

CONCLUSIONS

A major task facing maturing young adults is choosing a career path. Parents can help in the process by understanding their abilities and interests, discussing options, and directing them to wise counsel regarding options available to them. Then parents can pray with and for their young adults as they focus on this major decision.

PART II
Flying on Their Own
Ages 22+

THE PRODIGAL DAUGHTER
(Father's Day, 1984)

Do you remember . . .
    playing horse when Mom was
        at school?
    teaching me to skate and ride a bike?
    my first riding lesson on a horse
        named Clown?
    laughter and fun with cadets
        and friends?

Do you remember . . .
    when all that began to fade
    and you were faced
    with a frustrated, strong-willed
        teenager?

Year after year . . .
    you stood by and watched
    as turmoil and hatred emerged,
    yet you could not help.
    With each attempt to reach me
    I drew further within my shell.

A move to the coast . . .
    the path I chose worsened.
        Church, core group,
        my singing group—
    all a charade.

I played the part well . . .
    math, frustration,
        anger, arguments, tears—
    you saw the pain, but could not help.

Your wisdom . . .
    sent me on a journey to Bible school—
    the charade continued,
    frustration grew.

Parents weekend . . .
    I was alone—
    the pent-up pain and anger erupted
    and I broke.
    As always, you were there.

Could you see . . .
    the healing begin?
    the anger fading away?

My second year away . . .
    I'm homesick—
    I look to you for help and guidance.
    You are always there to back me up,
        to encourage, to advise,
    and to listen.

I remember . . .
    the times you were there
        caring, loving,
        hurting, praying,
    always there.

I remember . . .
    the many times I wanted to give you
        a hug,

to say I loved you and cared.
The many tears I shed
over arguments we'd had.

I'm sorry . . .
    for the pain I caused,
    for the many times I turned my back
    and said I did not care.
    I did care . . . I do care.

I praise God!
    for giving to me a very special dad,
    a man I look up to for many things,
    especially for letting me go
    so I could find
    my own way home.

Well, Dad . . .
    I'm home now; my wandering is over.
    May I come home?

Are you wondering . . .

what this is for?
I wanted to say
in a special way,
        Thank you
for patiently praying and waiting
for me to learn.

Most of all . . .
    this is to say, "I love you"
    and I'm proud to be your daughter.

Now I am praying . . .
    that we can be friends
    as God intended us to be.

Thank you, Dad . . .
    for being you.
    I love you very much.

                    Your daughter,
                    Karen Amy White

6

Letting Go!

Many parents would like to maintain control and influence over their adult children. It is difficult to see them make costly mistakes that bring them failure, pain, and suffering. Yet we arrive at a point in life where it's imperative to let go, mentally and in reality—for our good and theirs.

The Bible offers several examples of parents who let go and others who tried but failed. Hannah felt a sense of God's purpose for Samuel's destiny before he was even conceived. That purpose helped her let go and turn him back to God when he was still a small child. She let go even though she was barren and had no promise of other children. Although she made yearly contact with him, she still returned home shortly after seeing him, leaving him to the influence of the priest Eli and God. Can we in the same fashion let our young adults go to fulfill God's purposes?

Job prayed for the righteousness of his adult sons and daughters. He let go in a very real sense and simply committed his concerns to God. He didn't confront his sons and daughters and ask if they had sinned. Rather, he confined his uneasiness to his prayer time.

And the father of the prodigal son allowed him to

follow his own selfish impulses, giving him his inheritance knowing that it would be unwisely used, yet willing to give him personal freedom. He didn't try to artificially control his son, but let circumstances do the teaching.

When his son returned, the father met him with love and rejoicing, not recriminations. If the father had berated the son the moment they met, he probably never would have heard the words of confession and repentance. What did that ancient father do right in his difficult situation? He let go when his son strained to leave. He remained concerned throughout his absence. He watched for his return and repentance. He rejoiced in his son's newfound wisdom. He supported with love and commendation. And he expressed concern and recognition to his faithful son.

There is an old Yiddish proverb that says, "Small children disturb your sleep, big children your life." As parents we become so accustomed to the disturbances brought into our lives by teenagers that we fail to recognize when the results of those upheavals should be shouldered by our young adults and not by us. As they come through the teen years there are many disturbances, but then comes the time to let go.

Letting go is hard to do. An old song speaking of romance says, "Breaking up is hard to do." Well, it's hard for parents and young adults as well. Old habits are deeply ingrained. Parents tend to control. Young adults tend to lean on parental support. For the good of parents and young adults alike, those ties need to be severed.

Joan Beck in her newspaper column said this:

Do you do your young-adult offspring more long-range good by seeing that he faces up to the consequences of his behavior without your buffering? How much support and help can you give without sending the message that he is incapable of being a responsible adult or that his behavior isn't all that bad or that Mommy and Daddy will always be there to get him out of trouble, no matter what?

Parents never outgrow their long habit of picking up a hurting child (however old), soothing over the problems as much as possible and trying to make it all better—if not with a kiss, at least with cash or a lawyer.

And parents never outgrow the hope that if they just help this time, they will finally nudge their child into successful adulthood.[1]

Parents who release their offspring find a joy in watching them grow and function on their own. Much more than when we hold tightly, we see them begin to practice the principles we have been trying for years to get across to them.

The "open hand" policy frees both parents and young adults. When we clasp our sons and daughters with such force that they can't develop independence, we suppress their ability to grow into healthy adulthood. But when we liberate them, holding them in an open hand, they are free to flourish or fail on their own. When parents allow the opportunities of independence, young adults can accept or reject the responsibility.

As adults we understand the need to let go from our own experiences as young adults. If we know it, why then is it so hard to do for our own sons and daughters?

WHY DON'T PARENTS LET GO?

A father told us that his son had married at nineteen, against the counsel of his parents to wait a few years. He said, "One day I was riding in their pickup with them. And I told my son, 'Buddy, you may think you're in the driver's seat now, but I'm riding right there beside you.'" That father couldn't understand why we didn't agree with his attitude toward his married adult son. Not only shouldn't he be riding beside his son, but figuratively speaking, he should get out of the truck altogether.

But we could sympathize even though we couldn't agree. In a recent phone conversation with one of our young adults, we discussed five current issues in her life. Of those five, we wanted to advise and control on three. Reflecting later, we think we were able to restrain ourselves, but the temptation to intervene was strong.

Many factors prompt parents to cling tightly to their adult sons and daughters. Some are legitimate. Others are selfish. Whether for good reasons or bad, clinging will never forge healthy relationships between parents and adult offspring. The sooner we free our sons and daughters, the sooner we will enjoy new ease and depth in our relationships.

What is it, then, that causes us to cling?

Remembering Family History
All parents remember incidents from the past. We have seen our young adults make major mistakes. We have seen them suffer as a result of poor choices. We know their personalities and their tendencies. We dread seeing history repeat itself so we meddle and manipulate. With truly admirable motives we try to keep mistakes from happening a second time, or a third, or more.

Fear
It is a pathetic sight to see a parent paralyzed by fear. We may fear for the safety and future of our sons or daughters, or we may fear for our own reputation, which we have based on their performance. In either case, fear produces aberrant parenting.

Instead of trusting God for the outcome, fearful parents try to maneuver circumstances to produce results that will alleviate their fears. Fear causes parents to constantly interfere and to cling ferociously to their young adults. Fear, unchecked, has destroyed many lives—of both parents and young people.

Vicarious Living

Anyone old enough to be the parent of a young adult can look back on life and see blank spots. Unfulfilled dreams. Hopes gone astray. Unrealized ambitions. Failures. Broken marriages. Ruined relationships. Unfinished plans. Some parents refuse to let go of their adult children unless they will complete the dreams the parents have been unable to realize. It is a terrible thing to try to live life through another. Only God can give life direction. Living vicariously through a son or daughter will bring ruin and regret to everyone involved.

Anger

Some parents have been angry with their young adults for years. Young people passing through adolescence seem destined to generate hostility and anger in their parents. But if parents harbor that anger and let it fester, it will complicate a full release of their young adults. That anger will later be vented in unsuitable ways. Then only with help from God can the parents heal the rage and anger that has built up inside them.

One mother told us that when her son was a teen, she felt an increasing anger against him as he grew more surly, disrespectful, and argumentative. She called her husband at work one day and in all seriousness said, "You have got to come home right now and help me or I'm going to kill this boy." Her admission of need was the beginning of a healing process and today, several years later, that mother and son have a cordial relationship. The mother is praying that the relationship will deepen, but she has learned to pray and wait.

James gave us a clue about the negative side of anger when he wrote, "For man's anger does not bring about the righteous life that God desires" (James 1:20). This advice applies to the lives of the parents as well as their offspring.

Lack of Trust

Some parents never learn to trust God for their sons and daughters' future, and they certainly never learn to trust their sons and daughters. They regard every decision and activity of their young adults with suspicion and skepticism. They live in a gray world of mistrust, anticipating the worst from their young adults. They have never been able to convert their distrust to hope and confidence for the future. Old mistakes or even possible mistakes are treated as current events. Lack of trust keeps parents from freely letting go.

Parents in the process of letting go need a new mind-set. Young people *will* go, with or without our blessing. As we develop this new mind-set, it is helpful to remind ourselves, again and again, to trust in God, to hope in His goodness, and to let go.

When we are aware of possible mistakes, we can more clearly enlarge our thinking about letting go. We would like to elaborate on some of the blunders parents are prone to make.

DESTRUCTIVE PARENTAL TENDENCIES

Clinging

In the previous section we discussed why parents don't let go, and how clinging is one of the most obvious ways to hang on. How do we do that? One of our adult children said to us one day, "You're asking me too many questions. It makes me nervous. Why do you want to know all the details of my life?" We thought we were expressing interest, but on reflection, we realized we had gone far beyond casual concern and were meddling.

What parents regard as interest, young adults may interpret as prying. They may accuse parents of being nosy and snoopy. Young adults who are newly independent are especially sensitive to parental curiosity about their affairs.

Parents who control the urge to call constantly, to ask endless and detailed questions, have a better chance of ultimately hearing all they want to hear. Some parents insist on frequently seeing their young adults if they are in the same geographical area.

Of course, that can work two ways. One frustrated set of parents told us that their son and daughter-in-law lived only a few doors away. From their kitchen window they could see the parents coming and going. Each time the parents' car pulled into the garage, their phone would ring and the questions would begin: "Where were you? Who was there? What did you do? When are you going again?" The parents nearly went berserk trying to graciously field the inquisitions. Finally, they spoke frankly with their son and his wife, and although they were initially hurt, the questions eased and the relationship became less strained.

Controlling

Parenting is so easy when our children are small enough to control. Their activities, friendships, and moods are subject to our direction. As quickly as possible they should be learning *self*-control. Parental example and encouragement should stimulate their own control.

Some parents control with anger. Young people basically want to please their parents and will do what they're told in order to avoid confrontation or angry disapproval. Other parents make unreasonable demands on the young person's time and energy. Still other parents use finances to control—either by withholding desperately needed funds until the young person complies with their demands, or by giving money as a bribe. Some parents use guilt, saying, "We tried to raise you right. We spent lots of money on you. If you really loved us you wouldn't hurt us this way." Perhaps most devastating of all is control by the silent treatment. Young adults are helpless under such a tactic for it removes all hope of a relationship.

Controlling another adult always backfires. Each individual is responsible before God, and his or her conduct and decisions must stand or fall on their own merit. When parents control young adults, there are no winners, only losers.

Criticizing

Someone has said that one critical comment needs seven statements of praise and recognition to balance it out. Unfortunately, in most homes criticism outweighs praise by the same ratio. Even if parents haven't practiced giving praise and recognition as their children were growing, it's never too late to start. Young adults need recognition from parents. They want to hear that they are living a worthy life.

One irate father said, "My son is a fool. He can't seem to do anything right. I keep telling him how stupid he is, but he doesn't change." Even a rudimentary knowledge of psychology would have told this father that his son would live up to his expectations. And a reading of Scripture would show the father that he is completely wrong.

The Apostle Paul addressed this point when he said, "Fathers, do not embitter your children, or they will become discouraged" (Colossians 3:21).

Scripture reinforces the necessity for realistic encouragement, not frequent or unjust criticism of our sons and daughters who are taking those first formidable steps of independent living.

Is there something to criticize? Of course. They're young. They will make mistakes and bad judgments. They lack the reality of experience. But unless their decisions are life-threatening or blatantly sinful or unless they ask counsel, they must be allowed to make their own mistakes and learn their own lessons.

Who knows? They may be right and we may be wrong. After all, criticism is simply an opinion, not necessarily an accurate judgment.

Approving and Disapproving

It is possible for parents to destroy a young person's life by approving the wrong things and disapproving the right things. What do we mean? If we give our young adults the impression that we feel the most important successes in life are making money and finding a position of power and popularity, we drive them toward worldly, not godly, values.

If, on the other hand, we disapprove of their legitimate choices on the grounds that we don't like those choices, we risk destroying their confidence in God's leading. Several years ago, the daughter of some friends graduated from college and then, on a whim, chose to become a long-distance trucker. Initially, the parents were dismayed by her choice, but they held back their criticism. They realized that she had chosen a decent line of work that contributed to the good of society. She stayed in that job for four years, then returned to school for an advanced degree and entered the field of marketing.

By restraining the urge to criticize her choice, they kept the lines of communication open, and their daughter gained some valuable work experience that helped in her next career. In fact, her parents reached a point of pride in their daughter's unusual and successful choice of work.

Sometimes our approval or disapproval has its roots in our ego or embarrassment rather than in the good of our young adults. What if our son decides to spend five years as a ski bum? We may not approve, but is it wrong? What if our daughter marries an aspiring poet and lives with him in a mountain shack? Wrong? Not necessarily. What if an academically brilliant young adult opts to start a janitorial service instead of entering college? It is *his or her* choice.

Let's be very careful to approve and disapprove the right things. Of course, we want to disapprove overt sin. But personal choices, even though we consider them peculiar, are the perfect right of our sons and daughters when they reach adulthood.

It is imperative for their healthy maturity that they sense and hear our approval of them as loved people apart from their career choices, their marriage choices, and their life performance.

Manipulating

Manipulating is maneuvering and dominating another person by unfair means to achieve an end that is personally satisfying. Parents can fall into this trap by using any of the previously mentioned destructive tendencies. It's easy to begin to manipulate circumstances or feelings and then rationalize that we are "doing it for their own good."

Manipulation starts subtly and then grows to a gross parody of a healthy parent-adult child relationship. Letting go requires ruthless treatment at the first hint of manipulation.

Rebekah, the mother of Esau and Jacob, was a master of manipulation. Genesis 27 gives the pitiful story of Rebekah's favoritism of Jacob and her devious scheme for stealing Esau's birthright by deceiving his ailing father. After the deed was done, Rebekah further manipulated the hoax by arranging Jacob's hasty flight from his brother's rage. But as the story unfolds we see that the manipulation brought not joy but sorrow to Rebekah as she was separated for years from her favorite son.

Abandonment

Abraham tried to let go, but in actuality abandoned his oldest son, Ishmael, to the point of death when family conflicts arose (Genesis 21). By sending Hagar and Ishmael into the desert unprotected he was abandoning his God-appointed responsibility to them. Granted, God had given Abraham promises for Ishmael's future, but Abraham's rejection of Ishmael didn't help his son, and only relieved Abraham of a consistent, nagging problem.

Even though we reach a point where our influence is negligible in our young adults' lives, we must never indicate to them that we have abandoned our love and concern for them. That haven of parental warmth needs to be apparent to them even through the difficult times.

Destructive parental tendencies will devastate the relationships that we are trying to build and strengthen with young adults. If we are alert to the strong qualities of good adult relationships, we can stress those at the same time we guard against the destructive ones.

CHARACTERISTICS OF
GOOD ADULT RELATIONSHIPS

We spent an afternoon with four young adults, two brothers and two sisters, that we have known since they were babies. We asked them what they felt gave them such good relationships with their parents, even though they all now live away from home. Their comments were revealing: "Dad doesn't put his nose in my business." "Mom makes me feel at home. I never feel like I have to ask her if I can look in the refrigerator." "Good counsel is available, but only if I ask." "I can learn from Mom." "Dad encourages me to try new things." "We always have fun at home. It feels, well, sort of *warm* there."

Good adult relationships. They're so precious, but often so elusive. What can we look for and promote in our own relationships with our young adults?

Respect
This grows first out of a solid understanding of God's view of every individual. Each is valuable and unique, created and cherished by God. Can we as their parents think less of them?

Perhaps it's simple to respect our sons and daughters who have reached an exemplary level in their careers and personal lives. But what about those who struggle or fail or live foolishly?

A friend told us one time that if we can't find any other reason to respect an individual, we can honor and respect them because God gave them life. That's a starting point for respecting our young adults. We can grow from there.

Privacy
In adult relationships we understand the need for privacy, for personal solitude and space. This is especially true in our Western culture. Young adults have a special need for "isolation" from parents. Parents naturally tend to inquire and probe, but a growing relationship with adult sons and daughters demands that we free them from inquisitions. We certainly wouldn't appreciate constant inquiries from them about our activities, and they don't appreciate it either.

Friendship

Families are forever. All other adult relationships are optional, but once we are a part of a family, that can never change. Friendship built within families lasts and gives stability to the lives of young adults. Parent-child friendships shield individuals from many of life's hurts and struggles.

One of our daughters gave me a decorated magnetic plaque that hangs on our refrigerator. It says, "A Mother Is a Special Lifelong Friend." The writer of that little statement understood the value of friendship between parents and adult offspring.

That doesn't mean that family friendships never falter. Of all friendships, those between family members take the most strain. We live so closely, and we have such long histories, that we are bound to show hurt, anger, resentment, and rejection. But if the friendships are strong, they will grow stronger still as troubling events are handled with honesty and forgiveness.

Friendship enjoys the present, focuses on the future, and forgives the faults of the past. Parents who anticipate a strong friendship with their adult sons and daughters will quite likely see that hope realized.

Parents can nourish all of the qualities of friendship that we cherish in our peer friendships. Not only will parents and sons and daughters be enriched, but future in-laws and grandchildren will as well.

Encouragement

Hebrews 3:13 tells us to "encourage one another daily." Every growing relationship includes an encouraging environment. It is the soil in which good relationships grow. Sometimes it comes merely by being together. At other times, it will come through a word of comfort, a willingness to listen without advising, a warm hug, a phone call, shared tears, or a small gift that says, "I love you. I'm thinking of you."

One of our daughters was visiting one afternoon. As we talked at length, she suddenly broke into tears and said, "Dad, I feel that you don't really approve of my decision." The decision she referred to had been made several months previously, and the thought that I might not have approved had festered in her mind for a long time before it came up in conversation. I was able to reassure her that, although at the time I leaned toward a different decision, it was not my decision to make, and I did indeed approve of her, and that she is loved and accepted.

Those who are *alert* to needs can give encouragement. When our young adults were tiny, a cry or a complaint alerted us that they needed comfort and encouragement. By the time they become adults, they've learned to cover their hurts with a pleasant social facade. Proverbs 14:13 says, "Even in laughter the heart may ache."

Let's be tuned in to the aches our young adults may be hiding and offer encouragement often.

Courtesy

We were spending a week in a distant city and were invited by a family we knew slightly to spend an afternoon with them. Three young adults—two sons and a daughter—still lived at home. It was a *long* afternoon.

The rudeness between family members never stopped. They interrupted one another, contradicted and corrected each other during conversations, and even shouted in point-less arguments. We sat in their midst in embarrassed silence much of the time. It was almost uncanny that they could speak so roughly to one another and in literally the same breath, turn and speak to us with calmness and respect. We left that home feeling as though we had been to war, and indeed we had. A constant battle raged in their house.

On that same trip, we spent considerable time in the home of other friends. They, too, had several young adults still living at home. The gentle and considerate relationships we saw there served as a healing tonic after the stormy afternoon in the other home.

The brothers and sisters talked and laughed together. The parents never changed their demeanor, whether speaking with us or their offspring. The atmosphere radiated love and mutual enjoyment. Perhaps the most captivating aspect of their family relationships was the fact that they were completely unaware of the warmth and strength of the kindness they felt toward one another. It was so ingrained in them that they unconsciously lived that way. There were a couple of disagreements during the time we were there, but when conflicts arose, the family handled them graciously and courteously.

Are we as parents as courteous with our young adults as we are with others? Are there areas of life that we need to improve?

We live in a culture where rudeness prevails more often than not. In a legitimate search for honest, assertive relationships, people have become aggressive and nasty. It takes conscious effort not to be caught up in the trend of society toward belligerent, rude behavior. Why is it that we tend to be the most discourteous to those we love the most?

Love and patience are the building blocks for courteous relationships. First Corinthians 13:5 says that love is never "rude." Let's extend that kind of love to our young adults.

Freedom
The friendships of little children are possessive and guarded jealously. Healthy adult relationships are held openly, and of course that's what this book is all about. But we can tolerate

one more reminder to give freedom and independence to all adult relationships. Control stifles friendship; freedom encourages healthy growth.

Love

"Well, of course, I love my kids. I'm their Mom, aren't I? What an idea. Every parent loves his or her kids." Certainly, we love our kids. But do we show it?

We like to give ourselves a "love exam" every once in a while, using *The Living Bible* paraphrase of 1 Corinthians 13:4-7. We ask ourselves if we are meeting God's expectations for us in demonstrating love as it is outlined in this passage:

> Love is very patient and kind, never jealous or envious, never boastful or proud, never haughty or selfish or rude. Love does not demand its own way. It is not irritable or touchy. It does not hold grudges and will hardly even notice when others do it wrong. It is never glad about injustice, but rejoices whenever truth wins out. If you love someone, you will be loyal to him no matter what the cost. You will always believe in him, always expect the best of him, and always stand your ground in defending him.

A tall order. Do our young adults sense that they are loved in this unreserved, practical way?

Caring

In all solid adult relationships, each person knows the other person cares. That care is like a strong foundation for the superstructure of the relationship. It may not be vocalized often, but it is obvious. It is confirmed by availability, encouragement, support, and love.

In her newspaper column, Ann Landers often ends her responses to readers' distressed questions by saying, "I care." Do our young adults know that we care? We may not be able to do anything for them beyond care, but that may be enough.

How do sons and daughters respond as we let them go? As they feel the release, they will acknowledge that freedom by responding in a new way, an adult way. It may take time, years perhaps, but the groundwork will have been laid for a new and rewarding relationship.

A friend suggests writing a "letter of release." He feels that it helps young adults to receive a written letter from their parents offering encouragement, spiritual support, prayer, and a release to their own adulthood. This excellent idea releases not just the young adult, but the parents as well.

Another mother took her eighteen-year-old daughter for a week-long vacation. During that time she told her daughter, "We're proud of you and what you have done so far in your life. Now Dad and I are going to turn you loose. We will be available if you need us, but we're no longer going to direct what you do."

CONCLUSIONS

As our young adults mature, we need to mentally take stock of attitudes and look for new styles and opportunities to relate. Encourage independent thinking on their part. Avoid the temptation to always rescue them. Encourage spiritual values by example and occasionally by appropriate words. Don't parent by comparison. It's tempting to say, "My kid is doing better than his kid," or "At least my kid isn't as bad as that one." Let's view our sons and daughters as unique, special individuals. Pray—for their righteousness and against evil, for their spiritual growth and against spiritual downfall.

7

Boomerang Children: They Return

You have just launched your last teenager into adulthood. The house seems serenely quiet and tidy. No more towels on the bathroom floor. No more thumping music from behind closed bedroom doors. No more empty milk cartons replaced in the refrigerator. No more long, long, *long* phone calls in hushed voices punctuated with giggles or guffaws. No more crowds of teens flowing noisily through the house, slamming doors, and chomping their way through the food supply like hungry sharks.

Then, whoops! With a ring at the front door all the peace and quiet changes. There stands your offspring, suitcase in hand, announcing with a grin that he is ready to move back in. Independence wasn't all he had anticipated, funds are short, his roommate snores and never picks up his clothes, and suddenly this six-foot son decides home looks pretty good. Now what?

More young adults are staying at home now, or returning after a year or two of college, or after several years of employment and independence than they were two-and-a-half decades ago.

Today fifty-three percent of all eighteen-to-twenty-four-year-olds live with their parents or depend on them financially while residing in college dormitories, compared with forty-three percent in 1960. Some kids aren't out on their own yet when they approach middle age: eleven percent of all twenty-five-to-thirty-four-year-olds live at home now, up from nine percent in 1960.[1]

In their book about young adults who return to the home nest, Jean Davies Okimoto and Phyllis Jackson Stegall cite the following reasons for this growing trend:

- The sexual revolution and later marriages;
- A rise in the divorce rate;
- Lack of role models and rites of passage;
- The economy;
- Young adults strapped financially;
- The designer lifestyle;
- Alcohol, drug abuse, and emotional problems.[2]

How does a parent respond? How do we handle the renewed pressure and the forfeiture of the privacy we have gained? Are strained relationships inevitable? Are there any guidelines to follow? Should we place demands on them? Do household rules change? Can we refuse to let them return?

The Bible gives us a story (Judges 13-14) of a son returning home after achieving independence. Years earlier, Manoah and his wife received a special message from the Lord regarding the future of the child they had conceived. An angel told them to set apart the child, Samson, from his birth for the special purposes of God. Manoah and his wife concentrated their lives on raising a boy that would meet the lofty revelations they had received from the angel. But along the way they discovered their special son's strong will and explosive rages.

When he reached manhood, Samson saw a Philistine

woman that appealed to him. He demanded that his parents arrange a marriage for him. (Judges 14:4 explains that God's hand was in the plan, setting up a confrontation with the ungodly Philistines.)

But during the marriage ceremony Samson teased his thirty Philistine companions with an impossible riddle. His bride, more loyal to her fellow Philistines than to her new husband, coaxed the answer from him and shared it with the villagers. In response to the deception and with the strength of God, Samson destroyed thirty Philistine men.

Samson's anger raged against the Philistines, and he turned his back on his new wife and returned to his parents. Imagine welcoming this furious, betrayed, hostile young man. His parents experienced a significant shock at his return.

As the story further unfolds, Samson is clearly a man of strong will as well as strong physique. He exercised that will frequently and often in inappropriate ways. His parents must have often questioned his behavior even as they acquiesced to his demands. It's hard to see how God could honor Samson as a leader in Israel, but in Hebrews 11:32 he is cited for his faith.

How would you respond to such a situation? And, further, Samson's parents knew that God was in control of their son's life. How much greater their dismay and disbelief must have been when Samson took a shine to Delilah. They must have despaired of his usefulness to the nation of Israel. And yet we have no record that they distrusted God during the whole process.

RETURNING HOME

Many contemporary parents see their young adults returning to the family home for a number of reasons. Some are unable to or refuse to accept independent responsibility. They can't make the myriad of decisions that independent living requires. They are baffled by the functional aspects of finding an apartment or a roommate, paying bills, finding adequate work, and caring for personal health needs. They may be emotionally immature or financially strapped. They may develop a dislike for undependable roommates and suddenly remember the comforts of home.

Some young people chafe under the real or imagined restrictions they live with during their late teen years at home. They can't wait to leave and sample independence. Often they spend the last couple of years at home announcing their desire to leave and the delights they will experience when they do. They long to make their own decisions without parental influence or censure. They idealize the prospect of independent living and their dreams are rarely tempered with reality.

But they quickly discover the advantages that home offered and back they come. One mother told us, "My daughter wanted to move out at eighteen, and we had lots of arguments because I didn't feel she could handle it. She tried it, but she moved back five months later, changed and content and appreciative."

Many young people return to temporarily base themselves at their parents' home between job changes, during college breaks, while changing roommates or making other temporary living arrangements, and during other short-term circumstances.

Our daughter and her husband lived with us briefly a couple of times while they were in transition between apartment leases and between an early career and graduate school. We thoroughly enjoyed the companionship and youthful exuberance they brought to our home.

Another daughter returned home after college graduation, uncertain about her future. After working, then traveling, then working again, feeling quite at loose ends, she joined a career adults group at church where she met her future husband.

These short-term, transitional returns usually prove smooth for both parents and young adults. They rarely last long, everyone cooperates, and as a rule, plans are already in process for an end to the arrangement.

But there are other more serious and ominous situations when young adults come back. Some return discontented, disillusioned, bitter, or broken by their own foolishness. Some come crawling home in defeat after a bruising divorce or a job loss. Perhaps their health has broken—either as a result of their self-abuse with drugs or alcohol, or by disease. Some parents have received their sons and daughters into their homes after a stay in a mental hospital or prison. Sometimes they return home bringing a small child or two with them.

A father told us of the return of his daughter after a year of college. A strong Christian when she left home, she had been drawn into a circle of students who experimented freely with drugs and immorality. She had lost her ability to study, became pregnant twice (aborting the babies both times), and finally, broken in intellect and emotions, she crept home to try to find some value in her life.

Her parents welcomed her and put their own lives on hold for a year while they guided her back to some semblance of normalcy. But as the father said, "We had to postpone vacations, visits with friends, in essence, our future, while we helped her. We devoted ourselves to her for a full year. And it wasn't easy. We had to deal with resentment against her for what she had done to herself and to us. We were angry at times, and that alternated with deep sorrow for what she had done to her life. And often we felt guilt that we had failed her in some way."

A mother told us the tragic story of her oldest son. He entered a prestigious university on a full scholarship to study math. During his junior year he overdosed on drugs. He didn't die, but the high hopes and aspirations with which he entered the university were shattered. He is now twenty-nine and sits at home day after day strumming a guitar and occasionally tinkering with a car he bought as a teenager. Although he participates in a state-sponsored rehabilitation program, any promise of full recovery is nil. His mother said, "I work full-time because we need the money, and sometimes I dread coming home. It almost kills me to see my son. Such a waste."

When these broken sons and daughters seek to come home, their wounded spirits need more than a sheltering roof and occasional meals. They need sympathetic listening, understanding, and a refuge while they regroup. They yearn for parents who will identify with them publicly and privately, regardless of their conduct.

One parent told us that he swallowed his pride as he walked into church with his son whose ear was newly pierced, with an earring in place. Then he did the same when his son double-pierced both ears. He determined to thank God that his son was in church, pierced ears or not.

Young adults who return home don't need recriminations or advice—certainly not at first. The time for counsel will come later but first comes a period of acceptance—not approval of the situation that brought them home, but acceptance and unqualified love for them as persons. They need to feel valued as persons before a spiritual, emotional, and physical restoration can begin. Parents are in a position to provide that sense of value.

It's easy to say "accept and love" but very difficult to do so when the disappointment has been great. Only God can enable us to find that delicate balance between acceptance and criticism. It can be a time of deep spiritual work in the lives of parents, as they seek God's help in a way they never needed it before.

If parents can enter into the suffering of their broken young adults, acceptance will be easier. They have lost their independence and along with it, their self-respect. Feel with them. Imagine yourself in their place—dependent, powerless, weak, failing. Ask God for empathy and ideas to participate in their personal and spiritual renewal.

Psalm 147:3 tells us what God does for His children: "He heals the brokenhearted and binds up their wounds." If they will let us, can we do any less for the children He has given us?

Most of the time when we welcome returning sons or daughters, their situations won't be dramatic or tragic. They will usually return home for a variety of functional and legitimate reasons. Whether for a temporary or extended period, whether for positive or adverse reasons, adult sons and daughters do return. Are there any guidelines that can make it easier for them, *and* for parents? We think so and would offer these suggestions.

GUIDELINES FOR RETURNING CHILDREN

Clarify the Situation *Before* They Move In
Hoping for the best usually leads to the worst. Speak frankly together about expectations and apprehensions. Try to anticipate any areas of conflict and address those in advance. Discuss areas of dissension from the past and determine how to avoid repeats.

Define Financial Parameters
Defining financial parameters in writing will head off confusion before it begins. If you expect them to contribute to

rent, utilities, and food, discuss it before the fact. Have some understanding of their financial situation. This is a particularly sensitive area, and as parents we don't want to be overly demanding or lenient. Asking for financial responsibility in the household is not unreasonable, certainly not so if they are employed. You may wish to charge rent and save it to give to them at a later date if they are working toward specific goals such as further education or marriage. If they are ill or jobless, there will be other considerations, and their financial contribution will have to be deferred until they are able to work.

However, some young people simply enjoy the lifestyle their parents lead and want to participate without making a penny of contribution. One family shared that their twenty-nine-year-old son worked occasionally, but at minimum-wage jobs, and spent every cent on himself, his car, and his photographic hobby. They asked him repeatedly to pay a portion of his earnings for room and board, but he always had some excuse. Finally, in desperation and disgust, his parents gave him an ultimatum—pay up or find another place to live. He listened, promised to find work, but he still spent his days puttering in the garage or the darkroom. One day when he was out, his parents put his goods in several boxes, set them on the front porch, and changed the house locks.

They couldn't bear to watch his reaction, so they left for the day. When they returned late that night, the boxes were gone and so was their son. After two very long weeks, he called. In high spirits he said, "Dad, I'm working now, and I'm rooming with Sam. Things are great. I'll be by to see you this weekend."

Such a technique doesn't always have such positive results, but sometimes young adults need a nudge to accept financial responsibility.

Discuss the Functional Aspects of Sharing a Household
Do you expect them to contribute to household tasks such as laundry and cleaning? If so, make it clear to them so they can decide if they want to live under those conditions or not.

Consider the following things:

Phone use. Should there be limitations? Who pays for long-distance calls? Do they pay part of the monthly charges? Consider installing another line at their expense if your son or daughter will be using a phone frequently for social or business calls.

Parties. You may be accustomed to a quiet, reserved lifestyle, but your returning young adult leads an active, gregarious life. Decide in advance how much social activity you want in your home and discuss it openly.

Entertainment equipment. How often do you watch television? Do you want that standard maintained when your son or daughter arrives? What about the decibel level and style of music? Decide together to minimize dissension.

Cars. Do they have a car of their own? Do you plan to share your car with them? If so, will they bear expenses, including increased insurance?

Schedules. Do you want to establish meal times? Should they come and go as they please, responsible for their own meals? Would you prefer to have some idea of their comings and goings? Remember, they are adults and need the space and independence that adults deserve. But courtesy demands that they have some idea where you will be and when, and you should know the same about them to relay messages and keep in reasonable contact.

Consider Younger Siblings
Younger brothers and sisters need to feel that they are paramount in the parents' attentions and concern. This is especially true when the returning adult is burdened with prob-

lems. That older sibling has had the best of your parenting during his or her growing years and must not sap your emotional energy to the point that the younger children suffer as a result.

Consider the example the older brother or sister will set for younger siblings. Feel free to insist upon certain standards so that the lifestyle of the young adult doesn't adversely affect younger brothers and sisters. They need to understand that in some ways they are guests. It is truly the home of the younger siblings, and they have precedence over the parents' time and energies.

On the other hand, some returning young adults influence younger siblings positively, and their presence in the home is a reinforcement of the parents' leadership.

Continue to Lead Your Own Life
Young adults do not need to be entertained. They are more comfortable if they can determine their own schedule without feeling that parents will question or feel obligated to fit in with them. Continue to see friends, meet social and occupational demands, pursue personal interests, and remain active in spiritual endeavors.

There is no need for excessive concessions to them. They will be more comfortable knowing they aren't intruding on a normal schedule. Parents and young adults should lead their lives as autonomously as possible.

Plan for Privacy
Some homes lend themselves well to seclusion for family members. Others do not. Try to offer a place of retreat for your young adult, especially if he or she has been accustomed to living alone. One family in cramped quarters put a comfortable chair and lamp in their tiny laundry room. Their son would retreat there with his books and Bible to find his

personal privacy to the tune of the thundering washing machine and whirling dryer.

Parents, too, need privacy. Tell your young adult that there will be times he or she may need to catch dinner at McDonald's to give you an evening alone. Often the parents' bedroom will be a private retreat and should be treated as such by the entire family.

Avoid Directives and Control

Try to think of them as visiting adults, not children. Unless we have developed the mind-set of parenting *adults* (see chapter 6), we can easily fall into the habits of parenting that we used during their developing years—commands, rules, criticism, manipulation, or whatever our style might have been. It's time to set aside earlier parent-child strategies. They simply won't work with adults. They will be demeaning to our sons and daughters and frustrating for us.

Remember, It Is *Your* Home

They are free to accept your standards, or to venture out again on their own. This doesn't mean that we enforce rigid standards to ensure our personal comfort, but rather that we maintain a quality of life that has become our established style of living.

Since it is the parents' home, they have the right and the responsibility to set the spiritual tone. If a son or daughter breaks a moral or ethical code while living with us, we have an obligation not just as parents but as Christians to confront that action. In Galatians 6:1, Paul insists on such confrontation: "Brothers, if someone is caught in a sin, you who are spiritual should restore him gently."

What if the returning son or daughter is not a Christian or is living in a spiritually rebellious state? Parents still have an obligation to set standards in their home that they can live with comfortably, and then allow the young adult to decide if he or she can live with those standards. One family's oldest son returned home bringing with him a girlfriend. When he indicated they would need only one room, his parents informed him that they could not accept that arrangement in their home. He and the girl were welcome to stay but only in separate rooms. The son and girlfriend decided to look elsewhere for a place to live.

Grandchildren Return

Complications enter when a son or daughter returns with a child or two of his or her own. Who corrects the child? What if the child is troubled and destructive? Are grandparents expected to baby-sit? What if the discipline is harsh or even abusive? Again, the same principles apply as when just the son or daughter returns. Set parameters in advance. Discuss the contribution you are willing to make to the returning family. Adjust the home for the presence of a small child. Consider and discuss the length of stay as well as individual responsibilities.

When parents evaluate the return of their adult children, they must feel the freedom to say no. Parents are not obligated to allow a son or daughter to come back. Perhaps parents can foresee a negative effect on younger siblings still at home. Or parents might reject the return on the basis of past behavior and experience. And if parents choose not to open their home to a returning son or daughter, they need feel no guilt if the decision is based on sound principles and much prayer.

Some of the preceding suggestions may seem to concentrate on the problems of returning adult children. However, we want to emphasize the joys as well as the potential difficulties. Parents who have felt an unfinished relationship with their adult offspring have a second chance to develop a mature friendship devoid of the strains that directive and corrective parenting place on a relationship. It is a time for learning new ways to communicate, to discover what kind of a person your son or daughter has become. Parents often appreciate the companionship of another adult in the home.

Since Jerry travels a good deal in his work, having one of our young adults here is a pleasure for me. It means another voice in the house, a companionable conversation at the dinner table, and stimulating fellowship in the home—even someone to feed the dog when I travel too.

Parents have a chance to consider ways to make a contribution to the lives of their sons or daughters. Some may need encouragement—a small word of commendation, a listening ear, a thoughtful gift, a hug, a flower on the bedside table, or a prayer partner during difficult times.

At this point of life, young people solidify the spiritual teaching they have received into their own faith. Parents can have the joy of interacting with their offspring on a mature spiritual level.

It can also be a time of healing the past (see chapter 11), providing many opportunities to rebuild relationships. Young adults will see parents in a different light—as adults as well as parents. When the relationship shifts from parenting to friendship, parents and young adults alike are amazed and delighted at the change.

CONCLUSIONS

When we face the prospect of returning young adults, consider it an opportunity, not an interruption. Prepare to function together in an amicable way. Anticipate the chance to know them as maturing adults. Welcome the new ability to influence, and use the situation to reaffirm and spiritually influence their lives.

Welcoming In-Laws and Grandchildren

IN-LAWS

Recently a mother told us, "I can't stand the girl our son married. I've tried to like her and I pray for her, but she gets worse and worse. She's a greedy, demanding, immature person, always expecting us to give her things and make allowances for her nasty behavior."

We responded to this hurting mother with concern and sympathy until a short time later when we had an opportunity to speak with the daughter-in-law and son. Then we heard the daughter-in-law's side, "My mother-in-law is a witch. She's cold and selfish and critical. She talks all the time about being a Christian, but honestly, she acts like a devil. I will never be able to please her, even if we both live to be a thousand years old!"

As she spoke, we noted the look on the son's face. He looked withdrawn and weary of the whole thing. He had decided he could never satisfy either woman. It was dangerous to take sides, and his best action was to distance himself from the feud.

As families expand with the arrival of in-laws and

grandchildren, delight and enjoyment should increase. But sadly, such is not always the case.

The actress Cher said, "Some women get all excited about nothing and then marry him." Some parents feel that "my *daughter* got all excited about nothing and then married him." And, of course, the new in-law senses that attitude of disapproval, and the course of the relationship is set.

As our daughters and sons reach adulthood and their dating friendships take serious turns, we need to be prepared with guidelines that will govern our responses to both joys and disappointments. We hope and pray that our young adults will marry for a long and satisfying lifetime together. Some parents have been praying that for their offspring since they were in the cradle. But wrong choices and disappointments happen.

When parents make mistakes in the early days of relationships with future in-laws, the wounds may take years to heal, or even last a lifetime. Then, rather than joy, there is discord. Instead of friendship, there is bitterness.

Well, then, aren't parents allowed to respond to the choices their sons and daughters make? What if they never ask for counsel? What if it is obvious that the person they have chosen is the wrong one, for spiritual or moral or practical reasons? It would be so easy if we could make the choices for them as parents in some cultures have done in the past and continue to do.

In his fine book about Japan, veteran missionary Bob Boardman describes marriage customs in Japan:

Even in overwhelmingly modern and progressive Japan, with its ever-widening generation gaps and the erosion of the traditional family system, the time-honored custom of matchmaking still exists.

Omiai (literally, "mutual seeing") has recently

dressed itself in some stylish new clothes. "My Mate" and "Green Family" are but two professional marriage clubs, representative of over five thousand quite profitable marriage companies that network all over Japan.

The actual *omiai* usually takes place nowadays in a nice restaurant where the young woman and man can be seen sitting shyly and nervously with one or both parents and the matchmaker. If things go well initially, just the two of them will plan a date. . . . Either party can refuse or back out at any time prior to the actual engagement, where the match is sealed by the exchange of gifts between families.

Statistics show that *omiai* marriages are more stable, with fewer divorces. In view of these figures, contrasted with America's high divorce rate, perhaps there is truth in the Oriental proverb, "In Asia a cold pot is put on the stove and allowed to simmer until it becomes hot. In the West a boiling pot is taken off the stove and allowed to grow cold."[1]

Many parents in our culture would embrace the opportunity to get involved in choosing the mate of their **young** adult.

A mother spoke to us about her youngest child who has chosen to marry a man twenty-five years older than she. He has been married twice before, has children older than his prospective bride, and is deeply in debt. The girl graduated from a prestigious university, holds an excellent job in the business community, and makes a significantly higher salary than the future groom. But of most concern to the mother is the spiritual gap between the daughter and her fiancé. The daughter trusted Christ as her Savior as a teenager but slowly drifted from her spiritual moorings during her young adult years. Her future husband adamantly declares his contempt for what he calls "the crutch of religion."

This grieving mother sees only heartache and disaster in her daughter's future, and she asks, "What can I do? My daughter won't listen."

Genesis gives the story of conflict between parents and son over marriage choices. Isaac and Rebekah's twin sons, Jacob and Esau, had lived with favoritism and competition all of their lives. Rebekah preferred Jacob, while Isaac was partial to Esau. The tension produced by this inequitable situation spilled over into adult life.

Genesis 26:34-35 describes Isaac and Rebekah's response to Esau's marital choices. It says, "When Esau was forty years old, he married Judith daughter of Beeri the Hittite, and also Basemath daughter of Elon the Hittite." Although he had been raised in a monogamous, God-honoring home, Esau chose polygamy with unbelieving women rather than follow his parents' example. And the result was, "They were a source of grief to Isaac and Rebekah."

The strain in the family continued to mount, and after Jacob stole the birthright from Esau and prepared to flee from Esau's murderous anger to his uncle Laban's home in distant Haran, Rebekah said to Isaac, "I'm disgusted with living because of these Hittite women. If Jacob takes a wife from among the women of this land, from Hittite women like these, my life will not be worth living" (Genesis 27:46).

Although Rebekah's suicidal threat may have been exaggerated in her desperation to convince Isaac to send Jacob away from Esau, still her statements give us a clue into the atmosphere that existed between Rebekah and her daughters-in-law. And there is no happy ending to this story—it grows only more complicated and sad as Esau finally comprehends his parents' rejection. Genesis 28:6-9 tells us:

Now Esau learned that Isaac had blessed Jacob and had
sent him to Paddan Aram to take a wife from there,
and that when he blessed him he commanded him,
"Do not marry a Canaanite woman," and that Jacob
had obeyed his father and mother and had gone to
Paddan Aram. Esau then realized how displeasing
the Canaanite women were to his father Isaac; so he
went to Ishmael and married Mahalath, the sister of
Nebaioth and daughter of Ishmael son of Abraham, in
addition to the wives he already had.

In a desperate attempt to gain his parents' approval,
Esau marries yet another woman. That is the last insight the
Bible gives us about this in-law relationship, and it ends on a
troubled, bitter note. The entire family was drawn into the
fray, including brothers, parents, and wives.

If at all possible, Christian parents want to avoid the
struggle and suffering that Rebekah and Isaac and their sons
endured. But many situations arise that present complications for smooth relationships with in-laws:

- Sons and daughters fail to ask for parental counsel
  on their choice of a mate.
- They choose a person with many complicating past
  problems.
- They select a nonChristian for a spouse and misunderstandings result.
- They divorce and remarry, leaving complicated or
  broken relationships in the process.

As new in-laws join the family, they fail to get along with
each other, or force a climate of competition. Then when
grandchildren arrive, the furor and conflicts escalate unless
something is done to diffuse the situation.

When the time comes for our children to choose mates, we need to remind ourselves what the Bible says about marriage and see it in the light of our young adult's experience. The very first instructions given in the Bible about marriage speak directly of the responsibilities of the couple, but also indirectly of the conduct of the parents-in-law. Genesis 2:24 says, "For this reason a man will leave his father and mother and be united to his wife, and they will become one flesh."

Mothers and fathers: back off when the young adults marry. They are setting up an exclusive relationship. We can influence, pray, and respond when asked, but we must take our hands off them and let them "cleave" to one another. It's helpful to remember these instructions from the mouth of God when we would strongly love to instruct and interfere.

Relationships with In-Laws
We would offer some general suggestions for developing relationships with in-laws.

1. *Never criticize your son's and daughter's choices.* Your young adults will never forget your initial criticisms. If they're obviously wrong in their choices, direct their thinking by asking questions that will allow them to arrive at their own conclusions.

Rather than saying, "You can't be serious about marrying that lazy kid?" say, "Let's talk about this. Can you tell me what you see for your future with him (or her)?" Rather than "She would never fit in our family," say, "What are the best things about her, and what do you see as possible problems?" Instead of "His background is terrible. You two don't have anything in common," try "Have you thought about the things you have in common and how they contribute to a long-term relationship?"

Sensitive questions rather than condemning statements

will, perhaps, allow the communication to remain open and will direct the young adult's thoughts to a realistic assessment of the relationship. Young people in love, or who *think* they're in love, often lack a rational approach to the relationship.

Critical statements will almost always polarize the parent-young adult relationship and often will force the son or daughter to side with his or her chosen mate. Keep the verbal exchange flowing even when strongly tempted to blurt out a negative assessment of his or her choice.

2. *Building lifelong relationships.* Once the son or daughter has chosen a mate, the lifelong process of relationship building really gets underway. The major responsibility rests on the parents to lead the way to developing the in-law relationship to one of friendship and intimacy.

I first met Jerry's parents at their home on a hot, muggy summer afternoon when their house was crowded with relatives preparing ethnic Norwegian food for dinner. Although I, too, had a Norwegian heritage, I had never heard of the food they were cooking, and I could have felt that my background was in question. But Jerry's mother made me feel welcome, showing an interest in me as a person. Never once did I feel that I had intruded on a family party, but rather that I was adding something.

Throughout the twenty-four years that I knew her before her death, I cannot remember her criticizing me. She often commended or complimented me. If she had negative thoughts about the way I treated her son or grandchildren, or the way I lived my life, she kept those impressions to herself. I realize that sounds idyllic and perhaps it was, but throughout her lifetime our friendship was due to her early acceptance of me. She allowed her son and me to pace our own relationship without interference or judgment.

3. *Acceptance of the new in-law.* No matter who the new

in-law might be, even if you think he resembles Attila the Hun, or she acts like a spoiled five-year-old, if you are ever to have a cordial relationship, the new in-law must feel your acceptance. You don't need to condone every behavior, or approve of every facet of his or her personality, but you must accept the new in-law as a valued human being. Acceptance lays the foundation for future love and harmony. If he or she senses rejection, it will only delay resolution and rapport.

Jay and Louise entered a second marriage for each and brought four young adults with them, two of them Jay's and two Louise's. Although the blending of the two families was surprisingly harmonious, when the young adults began to choose mates, conflict escalated quickly. Not one of the new family members liked any of the other in-laws. Every family gathering was filled with bickering, face-to-face criticism, and snide comments. Since the sons and daughters lived locally, they were together frequently.

At the end of one particularly stressful family gathering, Louise burst out, "That's enough! I hate the fighting and name calling." When she had gained everyone's attention, she said, "I can't imagine that anyone else is enjoying these times together. I'm just not going to put up with it anymore. Jay and I love all of you, and when we're with you individually, you're wonderful people. From now on, we're just going to see each of you alone. Call before you come over to make sure your brothers or sisters and their husbands or wives aren't here. It means we won't get to see each of you as often, but I can't think of what else to do."

Everyone left that day sobered. Through the coming months, the family never gathered as a whole, even at Christmas, but Jay and Louise had some peaceful times with individual couples. Although it took more time to see the young people individually, they continued to pursue their plan.

About a year later, one daughter and her husband

invited Louise and Jay for dinner. When they arrived they found all the other siblings and their mates there as well. The oldest daughter said, "We finally got together and decided we missed being together. We've still got some things to work out, but we're going to try."

4. *Practice tolerance.* Any prospective in-law responds to a nonjudgmental environment. Parents should be patient with a new in-law, realizing that the new in-law is feeling his or her way in a new situation, as one stranger among many friends. The new in-law is entering a new family, long-established with traditions, idiosyncrasies, habits, inside jokes, history, nonverbal communication, and a myriad of other details that make a family. The new in-law has to figure all of this out and then try to fit in.

When parents set a tone of tolerance, patience, and restraint in pushing for a fast assimilation, the new member is free to blend in at his or her own pace. Parents who have pushed, criticized, and demanded conformity find that the in-law resists. Who wouldn't? A new in-law may feel that he or she is entering a different culture, and to a certain degree that is true. Environments and settings vary from home to home. While the original family members read all the unspoken signals, the new in-law is sailing uncharted waters. Tolerance of the new in-law's habits and responses is vital if there is to be peace and acceptance.

5. *Don't offer advice.* If the couple asks for advice, move in slowly, always finding out their initial thoughts before offering suggestions. Keep in mind that they have a new, unique home of their own, and it shouldn't look like either home they have come from. They are a blend of what they have known in the past, what God will teach them, and what they will discover together.

Your counsel can be helpful when based on sound biblical principles, but only if it is given sparingly, when asked for, and always with an emphasis on their *mutual* decision. If only your son or daughter asks for advice, and does so frequently, that could be a strong clue that the new couple is not making decisions together.

6. *Extend warmth.* Every family's "affection level" differs. You may be a family that expresses warmth with lots of hugs, kisses, and physical affection. Or you may deeply cherish one another but in a restrained, subdued way. No matter. A new in-law can feel warmth and approval if it is sincerely in the hearts and attitudes of the new family.

A stiff-armed, rejecting tone can be felt as strongly as shouted words. And again, parents bear the responsibility for offering warmth or projecting coldness. You set the pace in guiding the new family member into the style your family follows. Keep in mind that you may be able to learn from that new in-law ways of expressing love that you had not known before.

The following diagram helps you to understand the complexities that enter family relationships when new members join. Notice the number of relationships that need to be established and maintained.

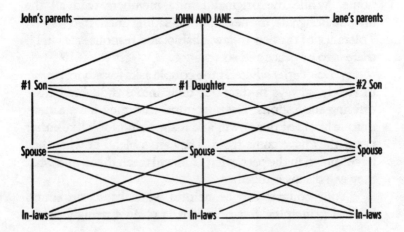

The interweaving of relationships is incredibly complex as the family builds. Pray for wisdom in developing all of the relationships, and pray for peace in the family. Then ask God for creative ideas in blending the whole together.

Some parents face a different situation. Their son or daughter may date a person they consider eminently qualified to join the family. And then a breakup occurs. Again, it is the obligation of the parents to support and affirm their son or daughter while swallowing the disappointment. Perhaps God has another, more fitting mate in mind for him or her, or God may be sparing him or her some sorrow or trouble in the future.

Conclusions

Parents bear the responsibility for acceptance, tolerance, patience, and warmth in the in-law relationship. Strive to make new in-laws comfortable. Don't keep score on the time they spend with the other parents. Don't offer marital advice. Try to be equitable to all sons- and daughters-in-law. Give commendation and verbal approval freely. Avoid all attempts to control or manipulate.

GRANDCHILDREN

Alex Haley said, "Nobody can do for little children what grandparents do. Grandparents sort of sprinkle stardust over the lives of little children."[2]

The Bible phrases it beautifully: "Children's children are a crown to the aged" (Proverbs 17:6). What a lovely thought from the mind of God. Our grandchildren make us feel like kings and queens. They are delightful, precious subjects in our small family kingdoms. They are the "crowns"—pinnacles in the life of parenting. Their love and trust in us as grandparents is unconditional and adoring—

the ideal response of any loyal subject to the king and queen of their universe.

Before our first grandchild was born, we indulgently listened to those who had already entered the ranks of grandparents as they enthused about their grandchildren, displayed pictures, and even offered to show us videotapes of the wonders their grandchildren could perform. We thought it was all very nice, but slightly overdone.

Then, we joined the ranks of grandparents, and we can now keep up with the best of them! Truly, grandparenting is one of the joys of life, as well as one of the most important God-given opportunities.

One couple told us they watched a forty-five minute video of friends' three-month-old grandson. When it was over, they voiced the appropriate praise for the baby, and the grandparents said, "Isn't he great! Let's watch it again!"

When our first grandchild was expected, the entire family shared in the joyful anticipation. On the day of his birth, our family gathered at the hospital, along with his paternal grandparents. Because of some complications, he was born by Caesarean section. When his father walked out of the operating room carrying that tiny bundle, tears of joy spilled down our cheeks even while wide grins split our faces.

But that first rush of delight is just the beginning. Then we realize the opportunities for influence, reinforcement, and enjoyment without obligation and support without hassle. Grandparents can fill the emotional cracks in a child's life—left there by caring but harassed parents, or by unkind playmates. Grandparents can be a strong spiritual influence, fortifying the teaching the parents are giving. Or they can even provide a spiritual influence when the parents are indifferent.

We were staying with a friend when she received a call from her five-year-old grandson. The little boy's mother had placed the call after a tension-filled afternoon that culminated in an intense disagreement. Knowing Grandma might come to her rescue, the mother dialed the call.

After the call was completed the grandmother shared the details with us. The conversation went like this:

"What's the matter, Billy?" Grandma asked.

"My mom is being mean," he answered between sobs.

"Well, tell me about it."

"I want to go outside. Mommy says it's too cold and she took ahold of my arm with force."

"But, Billy, you know God is pleased when you obey your mommy."

"I know that, Grammy, but I want to go out."

"It will be nice again, soon, Billy. Then you can play outdoors."

"But I want to go now, and when I tried to go out, my mommy spoke to me in her outside voice." (Later interpreted to mean she spoke loudly.)

After a bit more conversation, Billy subsided and realized he could find something interesting to do in the house until the weather improved.

Although we chuckled over Billy's expressions, the circumstance revealed the opportunity for a grandparent to influence the child and support the parent.

We can influence the grandchild spiritually. Psalm 78 reinforces the importance of reviewing God's purposes for us from one generation to another.

> O my people, hear my teaching; listen to the words of my mouth. I will open my mouth in parables, I will utter hidden things, things from of old—what we have heard and known, what our fathers have told us. We will not hide them from their children; we will tell the next generation the praiseworthy deeds of the LORD,

his power, and the wonders he has done. He decreed statutes for Jacob and established the law in Israel, which he commanded our forefathers to teach their children, so the next generation would know them, even the children yet to be born, and they in turn would tell their children. Then they would put their trust in God and would not forget his deeds but would keep his commands. (Psalm 78:1-7)

The benefit of telling our grandchildren about God is reinforced in Deuteronomy 4:9: "Only be careful, and watch yourselves closely so that you do not forget the things your eyes have seen or let them slip from your heart as long as you live. Teach them to your children and to their children after them." Multigenerational teaching serves to strengthen a child's faith and trust in God.

Marty's daughter married an unbeliever and had two sons. The father professed to be an agnostic and absolutely prohibited Marty to speak of spiritual or religious matters in the hearing of his sons. If she did, he threatened to never allow her to see them again. Marty accepted the ban, but prayed for grace to live the Christian life in such a way that her grandsons would see a difference in her life and be attracted by it.

On her oldest grandson's eighteenth birthday, Marty invited him for lunch. After a pleasant meal together, she said, "Gene, for eighteen years I have waited to give you the most precious gift of all. Today, when you are legally an adult, I can share something with you that I haven't been able to tell you since you were born." And she proceeded to tell him of God's priceless gift of eternal life through belief in Jesus Christ. Although he didn't immediately respond, Marty had the joy of knowing that at last she had the opportunity to spiritually influence her grandson's thinking.

When our sons and daughters are professing Christians and welcome our spiritual input to the grandchildren, we have a privilege to impact our grandchildren's lives in a significant way. Following is a list of effective activities that do just that.

1. Tell them Bible stories.
2. Recount your stories of personal salvation. Key them in to their spiritual heritage. If you come from a long line of Christians, share as many stories as you can.
3. Tell them how their parents responded to Jesus when they were children, if that was the case.
4. Pray simple prayers with them.
5. Tell them of answers to prayers.
6. Offer to take them to plays, concerts, and events of spiritual significance.
7. Give them Christian books, videos, and tapes as gifts.
8. Tell stories or read accounts to them of the great heroes of the faith through centuries past.
9. Speak naturally to them of God's blessings in your life.
10. Sing with them—especially little songs that are based on Scripture.
11. Let them share with you what they are learning about God and the Christian life.

Many of these suggestions presume that grandparents and grandchildren live in the same geographical vicinity. Even if you are distant from your grandchildren, use letters, the telephone, and tape recordings. Children love to receive mail and phone calls.

During the time of severe drought in his state, my

brother was driving along the road with his grandsons. They were talking together of the dry conditions when one of the grandsons suggested, "Boppa, let's pray about it." After simple prayers by all of them, they drove on. Thirty minutes later the rain began to pour down. "Boppa" was amazed, but the grandsons in simple faith didn't find it remarkable at all.

This story emphasizes another blessing of grandparenting. Our own faith is renewed as we see it in action in our grandchildren's lives. They pray simply. They expect answers. They never question the truth of the Bible. They hear and believe. We are spiritually encouraged when we see the family chain of spiritual links strengthened and growing.

If our sons or daughters are parenting alone because they are divorced or widowed, we have an opportunity to make a significant contribution to them as well as their children. Some possibilities include offering them a place to live while regrouping, offering child care on a temporary basis while they make decisions for the future, praying with them and for them, directing them to professional counseling if they need it, making practical contributions of home repairs, providing an occasional meal, and baby-sitting. Empathize with them, but always with a view toward helping them return to functional and emotional independence.

Conclusions

Grandparents have limits. Do ask for the parents' boundaries on what you can and should do for the grandchildren in areas such as food, gifts, and activities. Avoid interfering in their discipline unless it is abusive. Seek ways to make each grandchild feel individually special rather than part of a group. Pray daily for the grandchildren. Enjoy them. Influence them. Be their greatest admirers.

CHAPTER
9
The Power of Influence

Oliver Goldsmith said, "People seldom improve when they have no model but themselves to copy after." In the same vein, Albert Schweitzer said, "Example is not the main thing in life, it is the only thing."

The Bible gets more specific. Jesus said, "Come, follow me" (Matthew 4:19). It was obviously Jesus' intent to have a hands-on influence on the disciples. Example and influence have a profound impact on all of us, more than we will ever recognize or know. For young people, the maturing years are a prime time of influence, both for good and evil.

All parents want to positively influence their young adults. But this may not always be possible. As they struggle for independence, most young adults reach a point where they close their minds to their parents' counsel. They may do that in a rage of refusal to listen, or they may quietly follow their own preferences.

Parents panic when they see their influence begin to wane. First, we lose control and then even influence disappears. If our young adults are headed down a destructive path, our desperation increases. Sometimes we withdraw from them in despair and bewilderment. At other times we crowd into their lives with advice and criticism even though we know they aren't listening.

There is another option—the powerful influence of other godly adults. We have seen this influence at work in our own lives and in the lives of our maturing son and daughters.

We married during our college years, and as we recall, we didn't seek counsel from our parents, merely announcing our intentions. To their credit, they wisely withheld criticism, although they must have wondered how we would manage financially. It was hard, but we scraped along until Jerry graduated and entered the Air Force.

In our first year of active duty, two couples strongly influenced our lives, and the impact of that influence continues today. Fred and Barbara graciously befriended us even though they were very busy in a pastoral ministry. They spent many hours nourishing us spiritually and emotionally, even though they knew we would be in their area only a short time.

Bill and Doris met us the first Sunday we lived in their town, drew us into their Bible study, offered the hospitality of their home many times, and patterned godly parenting that helped us with our own young child.

Never do we remember either of these young couples, only slightly older than we were, giving us specific advice. Rather, they extended friendship to us, and as we responded to that kindness, we were influenced to a deeper walk with God, to more conscientious parenting, and to valued life goals.

All people are influenced by those they associate with. Paul writes, "Do not be misled: 'Bad company corrupts good character'" (1 Corinthians 15:33). And of course the converse is also true. We assimilate the good characteristics of the people we associate with. This is especially true of our young adults as they progress through the impressionable maturing years. Proverbs 13:20 says, "He who walks with the wise grows wise, but a companion of fools suffers harm."

For many years, we have prayed that other people would enter our young adults' lives and influence them in ways we could not. No parent or set of parents can be all things to their young adults. If they are to be complete people, they need the influence of others to help them grow into maturity.

As we pray, we are encouraged by the biblical examples of influence and the marked difference it made in the lives of young people. Where would Timothy have been without the profound example of the Apostle Paul on his life? What about Ruth? Without Naomi's dedicated and loving home environment, Ruth might have stayed in her own country, missing the great privilege of her part in the lineage of Christ. And Joshua? Could he have led the great nation of Israel in so many victorious battles without the time of preparation with Moses?

We realize that God can work when an individual is isolated—without the influence of any other person. But He rarely seems to do that. Rather, He shows Himself strong through other people in whom He is already at work. We are responsible as we grow spiritually to be a link in that chain of influencers.

PARENTAL INFLUENCE

Usually, parents will be able to influence young adults primarily by example. At times we will be able to converse with our young adults and verbally influence their thinking. But as with any other adult, we can't blurt out all we know or feel. And God can teach them without our trying to direct their every thought.

But God often graciously brings along another adult who captures their attention and affection and is able to share the things we long to say, to direct their thoughts and hearts toward God.

We first saw this principle in action with our son, Steve. Through his high school years and beyond, he was active with a group called Christian Service Brigade. The leader of the group, Bob, expressed his interest in every individual boy in the group. We had known Bob for many years and considered him a close personal friend.

One evening Bob arrived at our house. We invited him in, and although he greeted us cordially, he left us almost immediately and went to Steve's room where we could hear them laughing and talking. That scenario repeated itself many times. Steve knew that Bob was well acquainted with us, but he also knew, through demonstration, that he was the most important person in our family to Bob. Bob's concern and character impacted Steve's life in a significant way. Many times Steve would quote Bob's opinions and ideas on issues, spiritual and secular. And all of this influence was in the natural context of life. As Steve helped Bob with Christian Service Brigade activities, he observed Bob's active commitment to God and to people.

Together and with other young men, they had times of great fun. Bob was the first person, the only person as we recall, to take Steve snow camping. It didn't sound like much fun to us, but to Steve it was an adventure. And Bob didn't do these things from a sense of obligation or pressure. He genuinely liked the young men he influenced toward a godlier life.

We began to watch and pray for this phenomenon as our daughters moved through adolescence. And in every case it happened, in fact, usually with more than one person—sometimes a youth pastor, or a youth pastor's wife.

Or, in one case, an entire family befriended, influenced, and encouraged a daughter. We have been heartened and strengthened to see the effort others have made for the benefit of our offspring.

What, exactly, do we mean by *influence*? *Influence* is the capacity to sway the thinking or actions of another person without force and without authority. It is the capacity to indirectly affect another person using gentle persuasion and the impact of life on life. In its perverted extreme, influence is brainwashing. When the person is very weak, influence leads to disrespect and disregard.

So as we influence, and as we pray for others to influence our young adults, we want to see godly, direct, and positive action. Our young adults *will* be influenced. We all are—by every person we come in contact with to a greater-or-lesser degree. The power of that influence will occasionally determine life's direction for a young person. As parents review their own young adulthood, they can recall the many influences that impacted their lives. Some will remember narrow escapes from the tug of negative or sinful influences. Others will recall submitting to those influences with disastrous results. Reviewing the influences on our own young lives will help us understand the opportunities our sons and daughters have when under the influence of other godly adults. Although our personal opportunities are limited, parents still do have some opportunity to influence. They can influence their young adults in at least the following three ways:

Example

Part of the maturing process seems to be the necessity for young adults to mentally, and verbally, dissect their parents' lives. Perhaps for the first time they recognize our fallibilities. It's a shock to them to realize how frail their parents are as people, and often they concentrate on our failures rather than our strengths.

During this period of life we need God's grace to live exemplary lives before our sons and daughters. In the Sermon on the Mount, Jesus tells us, "In the same way, let your light shine before men [before your sons and daughters], that they may see your good deeds and praise your Father in heaven" (Matthew 5:16). If we are defensive or self-righteous, we will lose their respect and effectively cut off any influence. Our actions must speak for themselves when our words are not heard.

The strength with which we cling to our principles will impact our young adults. Notice the crucial word is *principles*, not prejudices or preferences. Do they see us living by a high ethical standard? Do they know that we love and honor God above all else? Do they know that we are generous, that we give freely? What about the use of our tongues—toward them and others? Do we criticize and gossip, or do we commend and praise? And do they observe by word and deed our marital fidelity? In these and many other areas they will keenly observe our actions.

Character
Although our example is an extension of our character, we can constantly check ourselves on the inner qualities that will ultimately be seen by our young adults. Certainly we want the fruit of the Spirit as detailed in Galatians 5:22-23 to be evident in our lives. We want godliness to be supreme in our character. We want to remain learners, willing to change as God and circumstances dictate. One of the most repugnant parental qualities to young adults is inflexibility, the unwillingness to admit wrong or to change. Our sincerity and consistency to deep values will capture the attention of our young adults.

Prayer

By far the most effective influence on our young adults is through prayer. Our reliance on prayer rather than our own efforts is a direct reflection on the depth of our faith in God. Are we praying with intense faith for our offspring? Do we believe that God will answer and work in and through them? Or do we pray with mechanical regularity? Or do we not pray at all, instead, working ourselves into a frenzy of worry? A few years ago when we were praying for one of our children, we were given a poem that has given us encouragement as we pray through difficult situations for our young adults.

Unanswered Yet

Unanswered yet, the prayer your lips have pleaded
In agony of heart these many years?
Does faith begin to fail? Is hope departing?
And think you all in vain those fallen tears?
Say not the Father has not heard your prayer,
You shall have your desire, sometime, somewhere.

Unanswered yet? Though when you first presented
This one petition at the Father's throne,
It seemed you could not wait the time of asking,
So urgent was your heart to make it known.
Tho' years have passed since then, do not despair.
The Lord will answer you, sometime, somewhere.

Unanswered yet? Nay, do not say ungranted,
Perhaps your part is not yet fully done.
The work began when first your prayer was uttered . . .
And God will finish what He has begun.
If you will keep the incense burning there,
His glory you shall see, sometime, somewhere.

Unanswered yet? Faith cannot be unanswered!
Her feet are firmly planted on the Rock.
Amid the wildest storms she stands undaunted
Nor quails before the loudest thunder shock.
She KNOWS omnipotence has heard her prayer
And cries, It shall be done! Sometime, somewhere.
—Ophelia R. Browning

MENTORS

Our parental influence may wane, but God often moves other Christians into the lives of our sons and daughters as friends and mentors. It is reassuring to see others step in and reinforce basic principles, be listening friends, hear them out on issues that the parents can't touch because of previous conflict, and challenge them to new levels of spiritual development. As parental influence diminishes, these mentors close a gap and meet needs that are unseen and certainly unmet by parents.

When one of our daughters was still in elementary school, she met Joanie. Although Joanie was a busy young wife and mother, she fit Karen into her life in a natural and loving way. Karen could talk to her about things she couldn't discuss with us. Joanie offered acceptance, love, listening, and respect for Karen. She was never condescending but built Karen's self-esteem and confidence. Together they prayed, laughed, and cried. The relationship lasted through Karen's high school and college years, and even now that Karen is a young wife herself, their friendship continues.

There is no adequate way to thank or repay these concerned influencers who without any reward move into the lives of our young adults. As we have watched them through the years, we have seen one thing they all have in common—an unconscious loving concern that could have been placed in them only by God. It's not easy to love a struggling adolescent or a rebellious young adult. But these faithful people seem to have an ability to overlook glaring faults and concentrate on the potential that as yet may be invisible to anyone else.

We want to encourage and enhance any positive relationship that our young adults develop with potential mentors. How can parents participate in such relationships?

Pray for Mentors

A mentor is a person, usually older, who becomes a friend and exerts positive influence and guidance over a young person. We have been praying for many years that all of our young adults would have such influencers. God has been faithful to answer that prayer at various times and in various ways. Pray, too, for those who are mentoring. Often they feel the pressure of being a model and counselor for our young adults. The responsibility they feel can be overwhelming at times.

One of our daughter's mentors called me one day and said, "We're really talking about some serious stuff these days. I don't know what to say to her. Please be praying." She did not offer to discuss the specifics with me, and I didn't ask. But later she called again and said, "Thanks for praying. Everything worked out great." Again she didn't mention the details, and again I didn't ask. It's important to trust the mentor, and to pray for God's guidance for them, and then to take hands off. We need to trust God's leading for them and to demonstrate that trust by not probing into the relationship.

Be Alert for Possibilities

We can foster relationships that the Lord may later develop into mentoring relationships. For a number of years we have been involved in Bible study groups where most of the participants are couples a bit younger than we are. Some of the deep relationships our young adults have developed have been initiated with those people in our Bible studies.

The purpose of the studies is personal spiritual growth, fellowship, and stimulation. But the benefit for our children has been an outgrowth of our relationships. The key will be a chemistry and an attraction between our young adults and possible influencers. Encourage that potential in any way to lead to the presence of a significant mentor in their lives.

One couple told us that they left a church they had attended since they were newly married in order to boost a relationship that was developing between their rebellious teenage son and the youth pastor in the new church. The pastor made regular lunchtime visits to their son's high school campus and showed a personal interest in him. After several months their son attended a youth party at the church and gradually began attending there. The parents moved in order to support the new influence that was directing their son away from evil and toward God.

Young adults need a person who will have a genuine concern for them. They are very sensitive to the sincerity of other people, seeming to have an instinct for insincerity. If parents push a relationship that has no innate mutual attraction, it is doomed to failure. The mentor alone needs to communicate the high value with which he or she regards the young adult. Any forced relationship is awkward, especially during the unpredictable growing years.

Never Intrude
There are times when we know our young adults are facing frightening issues. We may know of some, or even all, of the difficulties before them. And our hurting hearts ache to know of any progress they are making. But to intrude into

the relationship, seeking information that will bring ease to our worry or concern, will only result in a breach of confidence that could break the relationship with the young person's mentor. Trust God to work through that relationship without any influence or intrusion from you.

Eventually we may learn of the details, but perhaps not. It doesn't matter. If God is at work, if we trust the integrity and spiritual depth of the mentor, we don't need to know every detail. Intrusion brings distrust and probably disaster. Parents need to keep their distance.

Don't Envy the Relationship

For many years parents are the prime focus in their children's lives. They regard us as infallible, all-knowing, the center of their universe. Part of letting go (see chapter 6) is to recognize that adoration ends. Others become more important. New relationships supplant family closeness, and we naturally feel the rejection and hurt.

But if we stand back and look with rational eyes, we see that the movement away from us is healthy, natural, and right. At all costs we need to avoid envying mentors for their intimacy with our sons or daughters. They are providing a strong support that we cannot. They are giving input in a valuable way. They are a hedge against the immoral and evil influences that could impact our offspring. Rather than resentment and envy, we should regard them with thankfulness and relief.

After we have seen the benefit of influence in the lives of our young adults, we need to be alert to influencing the lives of other people in the same way. There are many opportunities available, and if we move gently into situations we will be available to influence other young people. They may be sons and daughters of friends, or perhaps nieces and nephews. The relationships may be short-term, or last for years.

My (Mary's) two sisters have given uncounted hours of love and attention to our children. And in turn, our son and daughters have developed trust and confidence in them, and respect for them.

These mentoring situations can result in chains of positive influence. When we were involved in the Bible studies that provided influence for our young adults, we noticed that they, in turn, influenced the children of our Bible study couples. It's a growing chain that will only bring help and hope to young adults moving toward maturity.

CONCLUSIONS

Other adults can step in and influence and mentor our sons and daughters when we have lost a hearing. Their positive and godly leadership can take over if our relationship begins to weaken. We can contribute by supporting and praying for those that God brings into the lives of our sons and daughters.

Facing Difficult Times

A recent newspaper article expressed the feelings of a mother living through a horrifying experience. Her twenty-nine-year-old son has been missing for several years. His former roommate has been charged with murder based on the discovery of her son's bloody clothes and car. As this mother awaits resolution of this dreadful situation, she told the press, "I've never been through anything so awful in my life. I feel like I'm smothering in my own nerves."[1]

Parents who have never "smothered in their own nerves" can consider themselves fortunate. Most parents of maturing young adults live through periods of apprehension, paralyzing fear, deep sorrow, or embarrassment. Even when we want to trust completely in God's goodness and control, our human nature responds to desperate situations with desperate emotions. One parent said, "It's much harder to trust God for my children than for myself."

Solomon understood both the pain and exhilaration of parenting when he wrote, "A wise son brings joy to his father, but a foolish son grief to his mother" (Proverbs 10:1), and "To have a fool for a son brings grief; there is no joy for the father of a fool" (Proverbs 17:21). Proverbs

23:24-25 also speaks to this point: "The father of a righteous man has great joy; he who has a wise son delights in him. May your father and mother be glad; may she who gave you birth rejoice!"

Although parents of young adults lead individual lives and follow interests and pursuits of their own, from the moment their children enter their lives as babies until they part in death, their lives are intricately woven together with the parents' lives. Their pains are our sorrows and their joys our pleasures. There is no way they can fully understand this connection, or be totally sensitized to it, until they parent their own children and young adults.

We live through it. We know the anxieties, exhilarations, pride, happiness, and grief that parenting young adults brings. We like to feel joy and pride in the progress of our young adults. But the hard times, the sorrows, the embarrassments, and the tensions erode our emotional stability and drain our spiritual reserves.

King David knew grief because of his offspring. When Absalom attempted a treasonous ascension to the throne of Israel and was killed for his treachery, the father-heart of David grieved bitterly. Even though Absalom had been estranged from David, had rebelled against authority, and had caused calamity for the entire nation of Israel, David's love for him caused him to sorrow deeply. David's response to the news of his son's death is described in 2 Samuel 18:33: "The king was shaken. He went up to the room over the gateway and wept. As he went, he said: 'O my son Absalom! My son, my son Absalom! If only I had died instead of you—O Absalom, my son, my son!'"

We sat with a mother one afternoon as she sorrowed over a son who had just been accused of several neighborhood burglaries and led away by the police. She was unable to speak and unable to pray as she sat with her arms wrapped around herself, rocking back and forth with tears streaming down her face. The pain in that mother could be tangibly felt in the room. She couldn't function, couldn't think, couldn't speak.

Few parents ever face such devastating emotions, but most will experience some struggle and pain with their young adults. And ironically, just as our sons and daughters struggle for independence, we may be battered by our own difficult times. Perhaps a marriage is breaking or we lose a spouse to death, and in our grief we must cope with the trauma of single parenting. Our elderly parents may need our attention and care, or our own health may decline for the first time in our lives. Women face menopause. Careers stagnate or diminish. Perhaps we have several children, and more than one may be struggling at any given time.

We could be called the "Squeezed Generation." Pressed by maturing young adults on one side and needy parents on the other, we also must try to attend to our own personal needs and adversities at the same time. The squeeze often occurs just when we encounter career or personal crises ourselves.

Allie was such a person. She made a daily five-mile round-trip drive to her ailing mother-in-law's home to care for her. The stress of the constant responsibility was taking a toll. Allie felt the pressure in physical and emotional ways. She had frequent headaches, her hands shook, and she cried easily.

Her two sons, one working and one in college, were spiritually indifferent in spite of a solid Christian home during their childhood years. Her oldest son, Matt, was living with a girl, and Allie strongly suspected that they were using drugs.

One afternoon as Allie let herself into her home after her visit to her mother-in-law's house, the phone rang. An impersonal voice from a local hospital informed her that Matt had smashed his motorcycle into a road-construction barricade. Although his injuries were limited to a broken arm, a badly cut shoulder, and a broken ankle, he needed someone to care for business details with the hospital and give him a ride home.

Allie rushed to the hospital where she found her son patched together and ready to leave. She returned him to his apartment, but by that evening his girlfriend had decided that she didn't care to nurse him back to health, and she called for Allie to pick him up and bring him home.

For the next several weeks Allie lived in a dizzy round of caring for an adult invalid son and a failing mother-in-law. She looked forward to the drive in the car for it was her only time alone without demands. She spent most of that time praying for relief.

Two days after Matt was well enough to return to his own apartment, her mother-in-law suffered a stroke and died. After the funeral, Allie suddenly found she had little to do. Her life focus had been her mother-in-law and her children. Facing exhaustion, she sank into a deep depression and for months received care from a sensitive doctor who recognized the symptoms and helped her back to physical and emotional health.

She slowly began to focus on the opportunities available to her. She started a Bible study in her church for elderly women and began visiting nursing homes, all in moderation, but with a sense of purpose and focus.

What can we do when everything invades our lives at once? We know that God is the answer to our dilemmas, but at times He seems far away and out of control. We see overwhelming problems instead of an omnipotent God. We focus on present problems instead of future resolutions. Help seems far away. Other parents don't seem to suffer as we do. We seldom hear other parents speak of pain that is in progress; rather, we hear of past victories. We feel alone, abandoned, and discouraged in the difficult times.

We want to sail through problems with confidence and spiritual victory, but our faith proves weak. It takes time to adjust to grief, find spiritual footing, and rise to a point of triumph.

Before that time comes, we may go through loss and failure. We would like to offer some definitions and some practical helps to parents facing overwhelming circumstances.

THE DIFFICULTIES OF YOUNG ADULTS

It's impossible to parent without visions of disaster creeping into our thoughts now and then. Healthy minds don't entertain the ideas for long, but all parents harbor a dread of possible disasters striking their young adults. And, of course, hardships and calamities will come, in varying degrees of intensity.

The difficult times young adults face fall into two categories: those that they choose to bring on themselves, and those that are virtually out of their control. Some of the problems that they choose to bring on themselves are:

- Rebellion
- Poor behavior stimulated by peer pressure
- Divorce
- Pregnancy
- Drug addiction
- Crime and encounters with the law
- Suicide
- Running away from home
- Homosexuality
- Promiscuity

Problems that are not under their control might include:

- Death of a spouse or child
- Accidents (auto, home, etc.)
- Serious illness, health problems
- Career failures
- Financial collapse
- Emotional or psychological problems

Let's look at a few of these in detail. We respond and react similarly to all difficult situations, regardless of the specific details. There are problems that impact us more severely, but God gives strength and hope for ourselves as well as our sons and daughters when difficulties strike.

PROBLEMS THEY CREATE FOR THEMSELVES

Divorce

Young adults may encounter serious marriage problems, even divorce. One couple told us, "We're so scared that our daughter and her husband are going to split. He works such long hours. They hardly have time together and our daughter is getting very frustrated. They're at each other's throats all the time. She doesn't have to work, but that doesn't seem to make much difference. We have tried to talk to her about it a few times, but she just tells us it's none of our business."

Parents feel so helpless as their children encounter marital problems. It is difficult to gauge the seriousness even when we see indications of stress and strain in the marriage. When we see problems, we may not be invited to share suggestions or give help. Often the help comes too late to save the marriage. Divorce may lead to loss of beloved grandchildren as a bitter spouse takes the children away from parental love and influence. Marriage failures bring pain to extended families, not just the couple involved.

When divorce seems imminent, we suggest several guidelines for parent interaction.

1. *Do not take sides.* Surely the fault lies with both and taking sides usually makes things worse. You cannot mediate when taking sides. You will naturally lean toward defending your son or daughter, but he or she is at fault, too. Rarely is divorce one-sided.

Admittedly, there are instances of abuse, flagrant adultery, or promiscuity when one spouse is clearly guilty. Even then, the rule is to save the marriage, not to lay blame. Particularly when grandchildren are involved, the offenses given in this time of emotional pain and conflict will color the relationship with the in-law and children for years to come, inflicting unneeded stress and consequences on them.

Try to see the issues from both sides. Objectivity is difficult for parents because love and concern cloud the issues. Sharing with a trusted confidant and listening to his or her perspective will help parents gain a more rational outlook on the situation.

2. *Be available.* Take the time to listen. For a period of time, parents may need to adjust their schedules and curtail personal pursuits in order to be available to listen.

3. *Encourage them to get counseling.* It is difficult for anyone to ask for counseling help, particularly men. Suggest this as early in the problem as possible. If the divorce does happen, remember that the children may need counseling also. Often their pain and emotions are hidden, only to emerge in the future. Children will try to take the place of the absent spouse in terms of responsibility and emotional support. Then if remarriage occurs, a new set of emotional problems emerges.

4. *Don't take blame on yourself.* In most cases when adult sons and daughters have failed in marriage or encountered

some other serious problem, the parents spend much time reviewing the past to see if they are at fault in some way. There are no perfect parents. Surely you made mistakes. You can admit them and ask forgiveness. (See chapter 11.) But don't take the blame. Your adult sons and daughters are fully responsible for their actions.

If they receive counseling, they will most likely look back to family failures and foibles, but that can only be for understanding, not for blame. If they try to place the blame on you, say, "I did fail you. I ask your forgiveness for failing you. But you are responsible for your actions today. You are an adult. You must accept responsibility for your own decisions. I will not."

This does not erase your pain, emotional responses, feelings of inadequacy, and sense of concern. But it helps. It begins *your* process of healing, for you are wounded too.

5. *Be a point of stability for the grandchildren.* Children are the innocent victims in a divorce. Before, during, and after the divorce they suffer confusion and deprivation and feel a deep sense of loss, often feeling at fault in some vague, ill-defined way. As grandparents you can become their point of stability. You can love them unconditionally, try to explain what is happening, and share in their hurt.

Grandparents cannot be parents, but you can be a refuge of love and stability, building bridges to them for the future. Particularly if they live with the parent who is your in-law, you will need to make extra effort to stay in touch.

6. *Be cautious in giving spiritual input.* In the turmoil of a divorce, reason, logic, and biblical truth often go out the door. Few people truly wrestle with the biblical right or wrong of their actions at the time. If they do it will usually be with a third-party counselor. If they ask, share the Scriptures with them. But until they do ask, save the biblical big guns until they are ready and open to hear. This is a difficult

posture for Christian parents who know the truth lies in the Bible. But without an open heart to God's teaching, resentment will result.

7. *Keep your personal balance.* During this time you will also hurt and suffer emotionally. But they need your emotional and spiritual stability. Read the Bible daily and guard your time of prayer. We recommend that you have a small support group or at least another couple or individual with whom you can share your hurts and receive encouragement.

It is difficult to generalize specific suggestions because divorce circumstances differ. The couple could be made up of two believers, or only one of them may be a believer. One or both of the couple could be adulterous. Physical or emotional abuse may have been inflicted. Or, one or both may be believers, but rebellious during the marriage. Each circumstance will require a different degree of involvement.

Rebellion

Many of the difficulties our young adults face result from personal spiritual rebellion. Even the perfect Father had rebellious children: "Hear, O heavens! Listen, O earth! For the LORD has spoken: 'I reared children and brought them up, but they have rebelled against me'" (Isaiah 1:2). And again in Hosea, the Lord's cry about His children sounds very similar to that of human parents in pain: "When Israel was a child, I loved him, and out of Egypt I called my son. But the more I called Israel, the further they went from me. They sacrificed to the Baals and they burned incense to images. It was I who taught Ephraim to walk, taking them by the arms; but they did not realize it was I who healed them" (Hosea 11:1-3). There is comfort in knowing that God has sorrowed through the rebellion of His sons and daughters. He can lead and comfort human parents as they do the same. Isaiah writes of this comfort: "He tends his flock like a shepherd:

He gathers the lambs in his arms and carries them close to his heart; he gently leads those that have young" (Isaiah 40:11).

Drugs, promiscuity, crime, failure in school, and even some career disasters tear at us emotionally as we see our young adult sons and daughters hurt themselves and others. It becomes a trial of faith for us as we stand by helplessly watching them destroy themselves.

One family watched, helpless and appalled, as their son slid further into a life of crime. He had been raised in a loving, attentive family and given many advantages, but as he moved through adolescence he grew more defiant, arrogant, and delinquent. Truancy and small thefts led to more serious crimes until the judicial system stepped in and threatened him with prison. His desperate parents urged him to attend a school designed for troubled young adults. He reluctantly agreed. After a year there, he joined the army and slowly began to rethink his mistakes.

What can you do? What actions will help rather than harm?

1. *Realize that young adults must live with the consequences of their actions.* Sin and rebellion always bring sorrow and hurt to many. When young adults do not immediately see consequences invade their lives as a result of their sin, it is simply God's mercy. How many times have we been mercifully delivered from the just results of our actions? It is always such a relief, but we cannot count on it happening. The Apostle Paul addressed this issue when he wrote in Romans 2:4-6,

> Do you show contempt for the riches of his kindness, tolerance and patience, not realizing that God's kindness leads you toward repentance?
> But because of your stubbornness and your unrepentant heart, you are storing up wrath against your-

self for the day of God's wrath, when his righteous judgment will be revealed. God "will give to each person according to what he has done."

They may suffer greatly. Yet it is *their* choice and it is *their* consequence.

2. *Wait with patience.* Parents suffer as they wait—sometimes for a long time—for their young adults to recognize their rebellion. Be there when they cry out for help and understanding. They may not use words to express their needs. Listen for that silent cry of anguish and cry with them. It may be years before parents hear that cry. Then, gently re-enter their lives with concern, not condemnation. They need to know you are there, not to rescue but simply to receive, and love, and help restore them.

3. *Keep communication open.* Letters and calls may go unanswered, but not unseen. Even when the atmosphere of communication is cool and strained, or nonexistent, you can keep trying.

Use birthdays, holidays, and special occasions to send cards or make calls. If rebuffed, do not rebuff in return and give them the "cool treatment."

One set of parents had no communication from a divorced son for over two years. The silence hurt them deeply. Sometimes they didn't even know where he was. They could do nothing but wait, cry, pray, and take the opportunity to communicate with each other.

Let young adults set the pattern for topics to discuss. Learn their interests and pursue those in conversations. However, there are times when direct, uncomfortable communication is necessary. You cannot avoid hard topics with a daughter pregnant out of wedlock. A son in jail requires honest communication on what to do. A crisis, as hard as it is, does suddenly break open communication. Use the opportunities wisely, with love and concern.

This is where husband and wife can balance each other. When you or your spouse slides emotionally and spiritually, the other can encourage and lift up. Times of concern and grief can intensify the love and care a couple expresses for one another. Use the opportunity to deepen your marriage relationship, trying to balance the sorrow brought from offspring with personal times of joy and laughter.

4. *Pray.* Ask God for another person to enter your young adults' lives and influence them in a godly direction. (See chapter 9.) Young adults can be vitally influenced by peers or mentors. They will reveal themselves to others in a way they never can or will with parents. Pray for the right influence.

Of course you will pray for their total recovery or restoration. Pray, too, for specific issues in their lives—the people who influence them, their jobs, their finances, their motives, and their spiritual growth. Pray specific verses of Scripture for them. One mother prayed Amos 5:14 for several years for her son who was living in rebellion: "Seek good, not evil, that you may live. Then the LORD God Almighty will be with you."

Enlist the prayer of faithful friends. During difficult times, selectively share prayer requests. Some people are more curious than concerned. When asking for prayer, do so from people who will pray consistently and faithfully.

Ultimately, the Holy Spirit will be the one who convicts them of sin and rebellion. Parents can be a means of help through prayer, but they cannot *make* the change occur. God alone does that.

Failures
William Brown said, "Failure is an event, never a person."[2] Even though our young adults will suffer failures, perhaps

frequently, as do we, *they* are not failures.

Young adults may fail in their education in small and big ways. They might elect to drop out of high school or college. Parents tend to panic when their young adults take a contemptuous or cavalier attitude toward education, because they know of its importance in our society.

One couple, both highly educated, told us that their son left high school during his junior year to attempt a career in a rock band. His high hopes were quickly disillusioned, and two years later he suddenly realized that he had squandered two vitally important years of his life. He managed to gain high school equivalency and enter a junior college, but years later he spoke with regret of his patchy academic history. He realized the lost relationships and opportunities that he had wasted in his fruitless search for quick fame.

Many young adults face pressing financial problems. Even working long hours, they can't seem to progress beyond bare necessities. Parents living comfortably resist the thought of their sons and daughters enduring near-poverty. Never mind that we lived that way ourselves at their age, and that they don't consider themselves hard up, we naturally want to pave an easy path for them.

Career failures aren't uncommon. Young adults may choose jobs that are beyond their experience or expertise. Or they may leap from job to job with little regard for personal advancement or employer-employee relationships.

Parents may see that their young adults never live up to their potential, instead staying in low-paying or unimaginative jobs, apparently content to settle for what we consider second best. Or they may decide not to work at all, hoping that we will continue to support them while they contemplate the future.

People who are not in tune with God's guidance systems possess a unique ability to choose wrongly in the major events of life. Our young adults will make choices that alter their lives for all future time. And as parents walk beside them, picking up the pieces, binding wounds, reaching out and being rebuffed, longing to help, they hurt with them.

Parents wish they could choose for their sons and daughters. We would like to roll back the calendar and rewrite history. We can't. We live with them in the reality of the present, with hope for the future, and with the presence of God to give us strength to go on. We do all we can. And then we let the young adults be responsible to do all they can. It is *their* life.

PROBLEMS NOT UNDER THE CONTROL OF YOUNG ADULTS

Many events occur in life that are totally beyond personal control. Long ago Solomon said, "In his heart a man plans his course, but the LORD determines his steps" (Proverbs 16:9).

An automobile accident can take a life or maim a person for life. Serious illness can invade the life of our young adults or their children. Emotional or psychological illness can strike in a debilitating manner.

Dear friends of ours lost a daughter and son-in-law in a tragic car accident caused by a drunk driver. Their two-year-old grandson was critically injured, physically and mentally. After the trauma that followed the accident, funeral, and initial medical care, months of waiting ensued. The hurt and pain were all there, but active involvement was not possible. The future fell totally in God's hands.

Month by month the child began to recover and respond more fully than anyone had expected. The process still goes on, deepening faith and trust in God in the grandparents' lives.

How Parents Can Help

When these problems enter the lives of our adult children, we have an open door to help them at many levels, even if relationships have been strained in the past. In some ways these problems are easier to handle because God's control is evident, though we still have pain and deep concern and turmoil.

One of the reliefs of these circumstances is that you can participate in the following ways:

1. *Begin to marshal prayer on their behalf.* Let the circumstances be known to close friends who will pray. There are times in life when you know you are functioning beyond your capacity, being carried on the prayers of concerned friends. Pray with certainty for total recovery or restoration. Pray for the young adults and pray for your own spiritual deepening through the entire process.

2. *Help your young adult.* This is a time to lift his or her physical load by cooking, caring for children, and doing other home tasks. One family told us that when their daughter-in-law was in an accident and spent several days in the hospital, they took several vacation days from their jobs, moved into the house, cared for the baby, cleaned, cooked, and left the freezer full of meals. Others were helping too, but they made the main contribution.

3. *Help them find the best care.* Often parents have developed a network of friends who can either help or direct them to the help of medical doctors, financial helpers, counselors, etc.

4. *Give financial aid and counsel.* You may not be able to help a great deal financially, but you can help them find someone who can give advice on financial planning or insurance, as disasters often place a heavy financial burden on the young adults.

5. *Help them think through their situation.* People under

pressure have difficulty thinking rationally. They respond to the crisis of the moment instead of carefully thinking of the possibilities open to them. Parents can help direct the thinking processes, suggest possible options, and listen to their plans. Avoid making decisions, but help them think through theirs.

In some cases little can be done after the initial flurry of activity. The task then is to wait, pray, and encourage. With God's help, time will be the great healer.

The waiting is hard. Yet in waiting, our character is deepened and our dependence on God becomes our refuge. Even though every person must go through the circumstances that God ordains for his or her life, comfort and help are available from God Himself, and from others in the Body of Christ. The Apostle Paul tells us to "Carry each other's burdens, and in this way you will fulfill the law of Christ . . . for each one should carry his own load" (Galatians 6:2,5).

Accept valid encouragement and forget critical comments. Some Christians take the role of "Job's Counselors" and are ever ready to indicate that any problems are the result of sin. One couple said that when their daughter attempted suicide, some Christians tried to lay the blame at their feet. They were mature enough to recognize that, although they had much to learn through the experience, she was responsible for her own actions.

Help for the Parents
When young adults face difficult times, parents do too. We want to participate in their hurts, then we need personal help as well because we suffer with them. There are a few key aids in that process.

1. *Continue in fellowship with God.* During times of trauma, we tend to pray more and read less. Sometimes we pray frantically about the problems, while neglecting to

listen to God's message given in His Word. Read consistently during the difficult times. When you're under deep emotional stress, it is hard to concentrate, so it may work well to read for short periods of time several times throughout the day.

Even if your spiritual life has been anemic up to this point, God is ready to welcome a new start. God is a responding, self-revealing God, always ready to answer when we reach out to Him, however feeble our faith. As the psalmist says, "Whom have I in heaven but you? And earth has nothing I desire besides you. My flesh and my heart may fail, but God is the strength of my heart and my portion forever" (Psalm 73:25-26). In Psalm 62:5-7, we find further encouragement: "Find rest, O my soul, in God alone; my hope comes from him. He alone is my rock and my salvation; he is my fortress, I will not be shaken. My salvation and my honor depend on God; he is my mighty rock, my refuge."

2. *Guard your health.* Emotional suffering often leads to physical illness. The stress of heavy emotions takes a toll on the body. If you are not aware and prepared, you can slide into physical bankruptcy. Almost everyone has had the experience of catching a cold shortly after an emotional time, even happy times like weddings and holidays. We don't rest enough, meals are hurried and ill-planned, we don't have time for relaxation and quiet, and soon we're in a downward slide.

Because you are aware of the potential of physical illness, you can take steps to alleviate this potential. Extra sleep, more attention to nutrition, a stress vitamin a day, and some time to relax will all give added physical strength. You will probably need to cut back on activities—saying no to optional activities, or even withdrawing from important ones, until the crisis abates.

3. *Have a group of friends to share and pray with.* Unless

you have this group in place before the problem arises, it is unlikely it will develop during the problem, at least not to the depth that you may need it. These friends will not be casual acquaintances, but people whose spiritual maturity has been proven, who are committed to faithful prayer, and who have been together for support, encouragement, and accountability. They will be able to support with prayer, wise counsel, and encouragement—essential support during the difficult times.

You will need friends who are so close that you can share anything on your hearts and minds—anger, sorrow, resentment, hope, despair. From a group situation, you may draw a few close friends who will be your confidants during difficult times. Relationships that allow and nurture openness do not develop overnight. You can prepare for your difficult times, and theirs, by cultivating these friendships throughout life.

CONCLUSIONS

When difficult times come into the lives of our maturing young adults, we can meet them with faith in God, the support of loving, concerned friends, and with a hope in the future. We love them or we would not be concerned. We desire to walk with them through these dark valleys of life in sensitive, practical ways. And through the valleys we will experience the living God at work in our lives and theirs.

11
Healing the Past

Memories of the past daily flood our minds. With almost every passing hour an image or event from the past interrupts our thoughts. Sometimes we dwell on them as we lie awake in bed during the night hours, or as we walk alone on a street, or ride in a car. Some memories give us a warm feeling of pleasure and we savor them. Other memories bring back feelings of intense fear or anger or humiliation. These memories often come from our childhood and our parents. Some of the most hurtful memories have been smoothed by the sandpaper of time. Some of the good ones have been magnified by repeated scrutiny.

Counselors and psychologists are inundated with people whose lives are permanently scarred by their past home environments and parental relationships. Without resorting to a psychology that blames all our present woes on the past or our parents, we do know those early events and experiences have marked us for life—for good and bad. There are the extremes of alcoholism, abuse, divorce, poverty, drugs, and intense conflict. But even when these extremes are absent, other parts of the past deeply affect the way we think and feel today.

The past is powerful. It confronts us at our most vulnerable moments. It controls us more than we care to admit. It fashions the way we think, respond, and act. At its worst it poisons the pleasures of the present and clouds our thinking of our future.

The most regrettable fact is that the past is unchangeable. It cannot be altered or forgotten, only examined, explained, understood, and reckoned with. God heals and forgives, but the events of the past remain unchanged.

But the past can also be a great encouragement. We can find many things to praise God for and to thank our parents for. Many people have a beautiful heritage, memories to be stored and cherished.

Certain personalities perceive memories differently. A person with a melancholic bent will dwell on the negative aspects of an event that overall was a good experience, while a person with an optimistic outlook on life will often suppress grim memories and focus on the bright recollections from the past. In both cases, the perceptions are probably distorted. Our memory banks are not necessarily accurate, they just exist.

What of our children? What past have we given them? What past are we creating for them now? No parents are perfect. Ours were not, nor are we. Most of us have already contributed the majority of our part to the past for our sons and daughters. And in that past we made mistakes—sometimes very bad mistakes. Some we remember all too well, while we remain oblivious to others that live only in the minds of our adult offspring. We are still building memories for our sons and daughters today—an encouraging factor in diminishing the negative influences of the past.

What can we do about these mistakes? They can be healed. We can deal with them in a cleansing and restoring manner.

BIBLICAL VIEW OF THE PAST

God understands the importance and impact of the past. He often reviewed the deliverance of the Israelites from Egypt. He chided them for the failures and encouraged them with their victories. As in Deuteronomy 8:1-3,11-18 (NASB):

All the commandments that I am commanding you today you shall be careful to do, that you may live and multiply, and go in and possess the land which the LORD swore to give to your forefathers.

And you shall remember all the way which the LORD your God has led you in the wilderness these forty years, that He might humble you, testing you, to know what was in your heart, whether you would keep His commandments or not.

And He humbled you and let you be hungry, and fed you with manna which you did not know, nor did your fathers know, that He might make you understand that man does not live by bread alone, but man lives by everything that proceeds out of the mouth of the LORD. . . . Beware lest you forget the LORD your God by not keeping His commandments and His ordinances and His statutes which I am commanding you today; lest, when you have eaten and are satisfied, and have built good houses and lived in them, and when your herds and your flocks multiply, and your silver and gold multiply, and all that you have multiplies, then your heart becomes proud, and you forget the LORD your God who brought you out from the land of Egypt, out of the house of slavery.

He led you through the great and terrible wilderness, with its fiery serpents and scorpions and thirsty ground where there was no water; He brought water

for you out of the rock of flint. In the wilderness He
fed you manna which your fathers did not know, that
He might humble you and that He might test you, to
do good for you in the end. Otherwise, you may say in
your heart, "My power and the strength of my hand
made me this wealth." But you shall remember the
LORD your God, for it is He who is giving you power
to make wealth, that He may confirm His covenant
which He swore to your fathers, as it is this day.

In this passage, God points out key reasons for the good
and hard times of the past. He uses the past to *humble us*, to
make us realize that we must depend on Him. He *tests us* to
reveal our hearts and develop our characters. He puts us
through hard times ("let you be hungry") to give us understanding. He wants us to never forget the past since He is in
control of it all. It is the history of God's working in our
lives. It is His history as well as ours.

In Genesis 37-50 Joseph had every reason to hate his
brothers, and even his father as he realized Jacob's favoritism
had caused the jealousy. Joseph was sold as a slave, deported,
and put in prison because of family hatred. Yet he recognized
it all as God's doing, "And now do not be grieved or angry
with yourselves, because you sold me here; for God sent me
before you to preserve life" (Genesis 45:5, NASB). Later, he
reassured his brothers with these words: "And as for you,
you meant evil against me, but God meant it for good in
order to bring about this present result, to preserve many
people alive" (Genesis 50:20, NASB).

Joseph came to grips with his family past—the feuds,
the lies, the deceit, the jealousy. Did it affect him? Profoundly. But he healed the past by forgiving his brothers. He
saw God using the very worst for *his* very best, and not only
for him but for many others.

The Healing of Recognition

We cannot deal with something we do not see or recognize. But once we experience an honest recognition of the past, we can then do something about it. When the past sits in the abyss of our mind, fuzzy and dim in reality, it festers and infects our ability to live in a healthy way in the present or the future. In relationships with our young adults, there exists a past that desperately needs to be recognized.

Recognize first that there are no perfect parents. We are all fallible, having made many mistakes in the past. We have a child and he or she becomes our first experience in child-rearing, an experiment in the true sense. We have never done this kind of thing before and enter parenthood with the naiveté of the untrained. We bring our prejudices and child-rearing folklore to bear on this new adventure into the unknown. Like a driver with no previous experience, we swerve and bump down the road of parenthood, doing the best we know how.

And many times, *not* doing the best we know how. For whatever reasons—personal pressures, fatigue, unresolved anger, conflicts with our mates—we expend our frustrations on our growing children even while recognizing the damage we are doing.

At each stage of a child's upbringing we make our share of mistakes. When our children were infants, we may have been too busy, overly permissive, or ambitious for their advancement. With our toddlers, we may have overdisciplined them or been too harsh or inconsistent. With our teens, we can recall myriad issues like conflict, disrespect, broken relationships, and mistrust. In the sixteen-to-thirty-year age period, we face many of the issues discussed earlier in this book. In all of these stages we made mistakes.

Now these mistakes are becoming more apparent to our adult sons and daughters. They have the maturity and experience to see our failures. We almost feel emotionally undressed by the exposure and recognition of our mistakes. At this point we're ready to look to the healing of recognition. Now we can recognize and admit some of the mistakes we made.

Take a moment to write down three or four mistakes you feel you made as your children were growing up that may now be affecting them. Just this recognition and admission to yourself will be a liberating experience. Did you discipline them too much or too little? Hurt them verbally? Ignore them in a rush for career advancement? Expect too much of them? Withhold approval? Spend too little time with them? Become angry too often? You may even wish to ask them what they recall or resent. But take the first step. Take the step of recognition and admission. It is the first step in healing the past.

The Healing of Forgiveness

Confession and forgiveness are the salve of restored relationships. When sin and offenses rest unresolved between us and God or our young adults, love cannot grow. If it does grow, it grows cold. Jesus tells us, "If therefore you are presenting your offering at the altar, and there remember that your brother has something against you, leave your offering there before the altar, and go your way; first be reconciled to your brother, and then come and present your offering" (Matthew 5:23-24, NASB). Seeking forgiveness is a necessary prerequisite to a close personal walk with God as well as to restoration with those we love.

When you recognize mistakes you made with your children—intentional or unintentional—first confess those faults to God and ask for direction in seeking your children's forgiveness. Then go to each of your young adult sons or daughters and share what you think you have recognized, and ask his or her forgiveness. He or she may have never given it a thought, or it may be the thing foremost in his or her mind. Ask if there are other areas where you may not have treated him or her well or have failed him or her.

Be prepared for some surprises. Things like an unkind word, putting him down in front of a friend, not commending her successes, unjust criticisms, and over-restrictiveness may be mentioned. Some of the smallest and least significant incidents may surface. Do not defend yourself. Simply say, "Please forgive me."

Often we're tempted to excuse our need for forgiveness by saying, "I'm sorry, but you made me mad," or "I'm really sorry, but I didn't feel very well that day." Such statements compound the problem and lead to further resentment instead of forgiveness and restoration.

At this point be prepared for anything. Tears. Silence. Disbelief. Hugs. Accusations. In extreme cases of broken relationships, your attempts at reconciliation may be completely rejected. You have now opened the door to deepening communication and to a healing of the past.

How does forgiveness heal? It is like cleansing a wound to halt the growth of more infection. It opens the way for the antibiotic of love to do its rebuilding process. Like the physical body, the relationship can rebuild itself with time. There may still be scars and scabs reminding you of the past, but the infection is gone. There is incredible relief and release in this cleansing, both between you and God as well as between you and your young adult.

Is this easy? Never. Asking forgiveness may be the most difficult act of your life since it strikes at the root of ego and pride. The process may be stumbling and awkward. But without it you will continue to live in relationships infected with the hurts of the past.

One mother of a young career woman said,

Ever since I can remember, I've been angry with my daughter. When she was growing up, I always seemed to yell at her and accuse her of bad behavior even when she tried to please me. After I became a Christian, I started to think about my relationship with my daughter. God finally gave me the insight to see that I was really angry with my own mother who had treated me the same way I treated my daughter. Even though my mother died fifteen years ago, I forgave her in my heart. Then I went to my daughter and asked her to forgive me. She didn't say that she would, but she didn't say she wouldn't, either. She's not a Christian and doesn't understand where I'm coming from. We aren't really close, and I can't blame her for that. I'm just praying that we can get closer as time goes on and that I'll have a chance to make up for all those past years.

Another parent, a father of several children, told us that he talks with each son or daughter as he or she graduates from school. He tells them, "I made lots of mistakes with you, and even though I tried to do my best I know I've hurt you. Please forgive me. I want you to have the best in life, and I don't want you to be held back because you resent me."

THE HEALING PROCESS

Healing is a process, not an event. Forgiveness from God is an event at a point in time, but healing takes longer. The healing takes place in us. As we admit and confess, a process of healing begins. It brings peace in our relationship with God and with our young adults. King David said, "I confess my iniquity; I am troubled by my sin" (Psalm 38:18). He also wrote, "When I kept silent about my sin, my body wasted away through my groaning all day long" (Psalm 32:3, NASB). When forgiveness occurs, peace replaces anxiety. The psalmist, after confessing his sin, said, "Thou art my hiding place; thou dost preserve me from troubles; thou dost surround me with songs of deliverance" (Psalm 32:7, NASB).

Parents are the greatest benefactors of this process since it revives us spiritually and gives new life to our relationships. The healing in us will take time. There will be periods of doubt, wondering if we did the right thing. There will be conversations with our young adults that may produce more pain as they begin to respond to this new communication from us. Years of irritation or infection do not disappear overnight. Let's allow weeks and months to aid in the emotional healing.

Then healing begins to take place *in our young adults*. Whereas we may have struggled with these past issues for days or weeks before discussing them with our offspring, it may be all new to them. Suddenly they find an open door into interaction with us that before was sealed and locked. We cannot underestimate their shock or surprise. They have not meditated on or thought through their response. Thus, their initial words and emotions will not always represent the best of tact and communication.

Their healing process is just beginning and their forgiveness may be partial. They wrestle with their own memories and hurts. They need time. We can nurture the process if we don't misjudge their first response. Even if they reject our request for forgiveness, we are still free.

At first they may even deny any hurt or offense. Conversely, they may bring up issues we never thought of. In either case, we are sowing the seeds of a wonderful fruit in their lives and our relationship with them. It needs space and time to grow while we renew our love for them.

Healing will also take place in our *sons- and daughters-in-*

law. This occurs in two ways. First, there may have been actual offenses against them—during the dating period, wedding, or early marriage. Since we are not privy to the pains and sensitivities of their past, we may have unknowingly hurt them. They deeply sense our approval or disapproval of their person, their background, their actions, and the raising of our grandchildren. If the primary offense has been against them, we need to deal with it.

Second, our relationship with our adult offspring affects their marriage in many ways. After all, they are more like us than anyone wishes to admit. They carry many of our faults right into their own marriages. When these issues of the past surface, they begin a correction process in their own marriages. They may see patterns they were unknowingly repeating.

We have often observed how many traits, habits, and prejudices we carried into our marriage from our parents. Some are beneficial, others are not. Our offspring do the same as they enter marriage. Sometimes they adopt a negative trait of ours, or they reject and overreact to a perceived fault. At times, our in-laws are deeply affected by this healing of the past. We can help them prevent a repeat of our mistakes.

After a stormy courtship, Fred and Lynn's daughter married a young man that they felt was totally unsuited for her. Lynn said later that she knew she shouldn't criticize him, but she often did in subtle, snide ways. Finally, one day about six months after the wedding, Lynn burst out against the young man in a blistering attack on his character, his potential, and even his looks. The young people left immediately.

Fred told Lynn that she would have to go to him and ask forgiveness. Lynn knew he was right, but said later it was the hardest thing she had ever done. She called her son-in-law and asked if she could see him. When he said yes, she went immediately to their apartment. Her daughter was nowhere in sight. Her son-in-law let her in and then sat on the couch staring at the floor.

As Lynn began to apologize, her son-in-law's head began to raise until he was finally looking directly at her. He graciously accepted her apology and from then on, slowly, very slowly, the relationship began to warm.

Lynn said later that she realized her son-in-law had always experienced rebukes and criticisms from adults, and he expected no less from her, especially after her outburst. When he realized she had come to apologize, he was amazed, and it was the start of a healing process.

Finally, healing begins to take place *between siblings*. As we bring the past to the surface we automatically stimulate a flurry of communication between our children. Some of our mistakes may have sown seeds of distrust, anger, and conflict between our children as they reacted and responded to our actions in their growing years. Each of them undoubtedly responded differently. They hurt differently. They handled the past differently. And, in so doing, they may have grown apart as brothers and sisters in some areas of their lives. This new openness could be key to healing and growth between them.

SIBLING COMMUNICATION

As our young adults mature and our influence lessens, one kind of relationship may begin to increase. As siblings, our sons and daughters will develop fresh relationships with one another. We hope and pray that these friendships will be deep and strong, and often that happens.

The first time parents realize their offspring are spending time together in activities that exclude the parents, they may be hurt. But ultimately we should rejoice that brothers and sisters find pleasure in one another's company, that they support and encourage and enjoy one another. That is a positive end result of relationships formed when they lived under one roof.

However, there can also be minor and major conflicts, and often the parents are caught in the middle. Sometimes young adults watch carefully to make sure that equality and fairness are practiced by the parents in all sorts of ways—gift-giving, time spent in each home, even the number of phone calls made to each sibling. This careful scrutiny of parents' actions may be rooted in perceived injustices from childhood. Or it may be simply that one child's personality has streaks of jealousy, greed, or anger.

Parents do need to be equitable in their relationships with offspring, but we cannot, nor should we, be equal in every instance. Life is not totally fair. There will be times when we need to give more attention and help to one sibling than to another. If criticism results, we can ignore it or use it to change in positive ways.

When siblings come to us with complaints about brothers or sisters, we need to follow the biblical pattern of encouraging them to confront one another in love (see Matthew 5:23-24). Openness and honesty in family relationships will always promote growth and harmony, even though the initial confrontation may be painful. Parents need to step out of the way and allow siblings to communicate and reconcile on their own.

PROTECTING THE FUTURE— LEARNING FROM THE PAST

The past and present intricately weave themselves into the strands of the future. No one can isolate and disconnect them. The trajectory of life and direction from the past possess a momentum that pushes and shapes the future. We *cannot* change the past. But we *can* alter its effect.

The book of Deuteronomy instructs us not only to remember the past but also to remember it in such a way that it influences how we live now and in the future. We must learn from our past "so that you, your children and their children after them may fear the LORD your God as long as you live by keeping all his decrees and commands that I give you, and so that you may enjoy long life" (Deuteronomy 6:2).

Proverbs 22:3 describes a naive person as one who sees evil and yet does nothing to avoid it: "The prudent sees the evil and hides himself, but the naive go on, and are punished for it" (NASB). When we look at the past, see our problems and mistakes, and do nothing to correct them, we make a grave error—in fact, we become naive.

From whose past do we learn? We learn from our own past—both our private past and our relationships with our parents. Then we learn from the past experience with our children. Take some time to think through some issues of the past. What are some regrets? What are some lessons? What are some issues that still seem to recur?

Goals and regrets do not change actions. We need to make a decision to change in areas that still cause problems with our young adults—actions, attitudes, habits, speech, and reactions. Most of us see our problem areas only in brief glimpses and then return to the blindness of habit.

When we identify an area where change is necessary, we need some accountability—someone to observe and critique us. In some cases, a spouse is best. In areas where family emotions run high, enlist the help of a friend. In some cases, perhaps even our adult offspring could help us and hold us accountable.

In all of this we may be tempted to think, "It's too late. It won't make any difference now. I won't bother to change." When we think that, let this sign flash across the screen of our mind: "Remember the grandchildren."

Do it for their sake. Let them see you change. Be an example of one who grows. Heal the hurts for their sake since the resulting pain *will* spill over into their lives through their parents.

ADVICE FOR PARENTS WHO FOUND CHRIST LATER IN LIFE

Many people come to salvation in Christ later in life, after the major input to their children has been made. In some cases, the history is ugly—divorce, infidelity, abuse, neglect, anger, custody battles, or ungodly behavior in the family context. Also, in many of these cases, young adults will not know Christ either.

The first step after recognition of the issue is simply to ask their forgiveness and take personal responsibility. Show how Christ has changed your life and given you a new value system. You cannot undo what has been done, but you can do right from this point on. Then say very little more for a while. Simply begin to order your life according to God's direction and let your life be an example. Begin to pray for your young adults regularly.

The greatest thing you can do is love them. Love them honestly and deeply. Love them when times are hard and when relationships are shaky. And *tell* them that you love them. They need to hear it verbally. Embrace them warmly. Give yourself to them.

Then wait. Wait patiently for God to work. Let them "see your good works, and glorify" God (Matthew 5:16, NASB).

CONCLUSIONS

Healing the past is vital for the future. We cannot deepen our relationships while the hurts of the past still have force. We must be ready to ask forgiveness, expecting nothing in return, but giving thanks when healing takes place. We can confidently do our part and leave the results with God.

12
A Final Word

Our young adults live in a different world than the one in which we reached adulthood. True, human nature remains the same, but the surrounding culture has changed radically. We were cocooned in a society where the external rules offered some protection. Certain niceties were observed; society forbade obnoxious or deviant behavior, at least openly. We were not persistently bombarded with the ugly, the sinful, the raw in life.

All that has changed. Because of the immediacy and availability of the print media, radio and television, and the close interaction with the shrinking world around us, we and our young adults encounter ideas and situations that would have been unthinkable a generation ago. Many parents choose a head-in-the-sand posture, hoping that what they see and hear really isn't true, and that their young adults are not really affected by it, if indeed it is true.

One person suggested that parents educate their young adults totally at home, including teaching a cottage trade, rather than expose them to life in the world. But, then, how can they be the salt and light (Matthew 5:13-16) that God wants them to be? How can they be "in the world, but not of the world"? They would live in an isolated, insulated world where no one affects them, and they affect no one.

Through this stage of our children's lives we want to have the best possible relationship with them. This comes about through a deepening walk with God, a better understanding of them, and a recognition of the forces in the world in which they live.

Review again the goal outlined in chapter 1:

> *Our overall goal for our sons and daughters is that they grow into mature, independent, godly adults*
> *who base their lives on sound principles,*
> *who are emotionally and spiritually strong,*
> *who have a strong sense of responsibility toward their fellowman,*
> *who will face good and difficult times with calmness and perseverance, and*
> *who, if married, become competent and faithful husbands, wives, and parents.*

Let's ask God for the humility to give Him the praise when our sons and daughters do well, and to refuse to live in guilt when they are struggling. With God's help, let's bind up the wounds of parents who are suffering, and strengthen the hope of those who are discouraged. With our faith firmly planted in God's goodness and sovereignty, we can meet the pains and pleasures that come with parenting adult children.

Endnotes

CHAPTER 3

1. Susan Littwin, *The Postponed Generation* (New York: William Morrow and Co., 1986), page 33.

CHAPTER 5

1. Littwin, *The Postponed Generation*, pages 14-15.
2. Littwin, pages 16-17.
3. *Occupational Outlook Handbook*, 1988-1989 Edition, U.S. Department of Labor, Bureau of Labor Statistics, Bulletin 2300, April 1988, page 9.
4. *Occupational Outlook Handbook*, page 28.
5. M. Scott Peck, *The Road Less Traveled* (New York: Simon & Schuster, 1978), page 15.
6. Peck, page 15.
7. Jerry White, *Honesty, Morality, and Conscience* (Colorado Springs, Colo.: NavPress, 1979), page 51.

CHAPTER 6

1. Joan Beck, *Dayton Daily News*, June 28, 1988.

CHAPTER 7

1. Denise M. Topolnicki, "What You Really Owe Your Kids," *Money*, June 1988, page 158.
2. Jean Davies Okimoto and Phyllis Jackson Stegall, *Boomerang Kids* (Boston: Little, Brown and Co., 1987), pages 6-13.

CHAPTER 8

1. Robert Boardman, *A Higher Honor* (Colorado Springs, Colo.: NavPress, 1986), pages 164-166.
2. Alex Haley, "The Maroon," *Reader's Digest*, December 1987, page 45.

CHAPTER 10

1. *The Denver Post*, September 3, 1988, page 5C.
2. "Quotable Quotes," *Reader's Digest*, March 1986, inside front cover.